Meet & Grow Rich

How to Easily Create and Operate Your Own "Mastermind" Group for Health, Wealth, and More

Joe Vitale
Bill Hibbler

16
EasyRead Large

RHYW

Copyright Page from the Original Book

Published by John Wiley & Sons, Inc., Hoboken, New Jersey.
Published simultaneously in Canada.

For general information on our other products and services or for technical support, please contact our Customer Care Department within the United States at (800) 762-2974, outside the United States at (317) 572-3993 or fax (317) 572-4002.

Wiley also publishes its books in a variety of electronic formats. Some content that appears in print may not be available in electronic books. For more information about Wiley products, visit our web site at www.wiley.com.

Library of Congess Cataloging-in-Publication Data:

Vitale, Joe.
    Meet & grow rich : how to easily create and operate your own mastermind group for health, wealth, and more / Joe Vitale, Bill Hibbler.
        p.   cm.
    ISBN-13: 978-0-470-04548-0 (cloth)
    ISBN-10: 0-470-04548-5 (cloth)
    1. Success in business—Social aspects.   2. Success—Social aspects.   3. Self-help groups.   4. Business networks.   I. Hibbler, Bill.   II. Title.
    HF5386.H48   2006
    650.1—dc22
                                                    2006008115

Printed in the United States of America.

10   9   8   7   6   5   4   3   2   1

This optimized ReadHowYouWant edition contains the complete, unabridged text of the original publisher's edition. Other aspects of the book may vary from the original edition.

ReadHowYouWant partners with publishers to provide books for ALL Kinds of Readers. For more information about Becoming A (RHYW) Registered Reader and to find more titles in your preferred format, visit:
www.readhowyouwant.com

TABLE OF CONTENTS

Additional Praise for Meet & Grow Rich

A mastermind group can be that elusive spark that brings out the greatness you know has been waiting inside you all along. This is the hands-down best book on the topic.

Mark Joyner
#1 best-selling author of *The Great Formula*
www.markjoyner.name

From kitchen-table problem-solving groups to telephone or web-based meetings of the minds, this book explains how to organize, run, and sustain a group dedicated to helping all its members succeed. Masterminding is a simple yet profound idea that can transform your life!

Marcia Yudkin
Author of over 10 books including
6 Steps to Free Publicity

Meet & Grow Rich is truly a road map to success. As Bill Hibbler and Joe Vitale describe, mastermind groups such as Ben Franklin's were responsible for major step forwards—like volunteer fire departments, the first library, the first public hospital, paved streets, and the University of Pennsylvania. THINK WHAT A

MASTER MIND GROUP COULD DO FOR YOU! Whether you're creating a local group that meets face-to-face, or a telephone-based group with members located throughout the world, you'll find the detailed information you need to succeed.

Roger C. Parker
$32 Million Dollar author and marketing coach
www.designtosellonline.com

Nothing is more powerful in creating success than a powerful mastermind group. Joe Vitale and Bill Hibbler have created the fastest and most useful method of getting your mastermind group to be smarter, more committed, and to get real results. Don't waste time trying to start one on your own, until you read this book. My mastermind group is now inspiring 1000s of Hypnotherapists and has accelerated their business and marketing expertise like nothing else could. The more knowledge we share, the faster we learn. Why keep making the same mistakes that others have made? Find out what doesn't work, as fast as you can! When you have an excellent mastermind group you can hit the ground running. This book is the fastest way to do it.

Wendi Friesen
The largest hypnosis resource in the world
www.Wendi.com

What you have just provided the world with *Meet & Grow Rich* is absolutely the most valuable resource I can imagine. This book is a masterpiece and will help so many people tap into the true power of the mastermind principle. Even though I've participated in a number of mastermind groups for many years I couldn't put it down once I started reading. Well-written, enjoyable, and bursting at the seams with practical advice, ideas, and insights. You have truly provided a simple and complete blueprint anyone can follow easily.

Rob Fighter
www.nohypemarketing.com

The power of the mastermind is obvious to me—I'm living it. I'm going to give a copy of this book to everybody I care about, and I suggest that you do the same. If you truly care for someone, buy them a copy of this book. What could be a more valuable gift than success, freedom, and wealth?

Pat O'Bryan
Creator of "Your Portable Empire"
www.Patobryan.com

Sometimes we can't succeed in life working alone. Instead, it's often helpful to surround ourselves with people who share a common purpose for complete and total success in life. In *Meet & Grow Rich,* Joe describes numerous proven and effective ways of using a "mastermind" group to greatly enhance your health, wealth, and personal power. This book is witty, powerful, and wise—and I can't recommend it highly enough.

David Riklan
Founder of SelfGrowth.com
The #1 self-improvement site on the Internet

I dedicate this book to my current mastermind members: Jillian, Pat, Craig, Cindy, Nerissa, and Bill. Thank you for being my support, my friends, my partners.

—Joe Vitale

I'd like to dedicate this book to the Wimberley Group (Cindy, Craig, Jillian, Joe, Nerissa, and Pat) as well as to Joe Gavito, Max Shuldberg, and Roger Igo from the Houston Group.

—Bill Hibbler

Acknowledgments

A book is never the effort of one person. In this case, an entire team was involved. We want to thank Matt Holt at Wiley, as well as his staff, Kate, Shannon, and Keith. We thank everyone who contributed passages to this book, who are named within. And we thank our partners, Nerissa Oden and Elena Hibbler.

Introduction

How do you achieve success in today's chaotic world? It often feels like it's you against the universe. But what if you had a support team? A group of people who could advise you, encourage you, and cheer you on?

Mastermind groups have proven themselves effective for everything from emotional support to financial support. Some of the greatest tycoons in history, from Andrew Carnegie to Dale Carnegie, have used masterminds.

But a mastermind is not just a support group. Nor is it just a brainstorming group. A mastermind has to have a single purpose to be a legitimate mastermind. What is that purpose? How do you decide it? How do you bring people into a small group that agrees with that purpose?

Key people have written about the importance to their success of joining a mastermind group. You'll find it mentioned in books by the legendary Napoleon Hill, author of the classic *Think and Grow Rich,* and *Chicken Soup for the Soul* creator Jack Canfield. You'll hear it mentioned on speaking platforms in seminars around the world.

But rarely, if ever, does anyone discuss how to go about forming and running a successful mastermind group. To many, the whole concept seems to be shrouded in mystery like a secret society.

One curious person once asked the authors, "Do you meet in robes, light candles, and perform rituals?"

Ah, no.

Then there's the confusion over the term "mastermind." It's often used to describe one person who is either exceptionally smart or exceptionally evil. Someone who develops a new field or plans a bank robbery may be called a mastermind. But that is referring to an individual, not a group.

So what is a mastermind alliance? And how do you create one?

Those questions will be answered in this book. Now, at last, you will be able to form and run your own mastermind group, regardless of your location, situation, or goals. Although primarily focused on masterminds for financial success, the techniques in this book can be used to form groups focused on fitness, hobbies, parenting, fund-raising, romance, spirituality, or any other area where people are seeking self-improvement.

We titled this book *Meet and Grow Rich* for a reason. Creating a mastermind can help you get rich in terms of dollars, and also in terms of happiness and lifestyle. Masterminds are limited only by your imagination—as well as those in your group.

Also, we titled this book *Meet and Grow Rich* in honor of a book from 1923 that Joe Vitale, an avid book collector and reader, found. It is called *Laugh and Grow Rich.* It has nothing to do with masterminds but may in fact be where Napoleon Hill got the idea for his book title, *Think and Grow Rich.* Many authors have been inspired by that 1923 title. Today you'll find *Publish and Grow Rich, Speak and Grow Rich,* and *Feel and Grow Rich,* among many others.

The point is, you *can* meet and grow rich—once you know how.

This is the first book in history to explain step by step how to create a network for success.

Are you ready?

If so, just turn the page.

PART I

1

WHAT IS A MASTERMIND GROUP?

Never doubt that a small group of thoughtful, committed citizens can change the world. Indeed, it is the only thing that ever has.

—Margaret Mead

THE HISTORY OF MASTERMIND GROUPS

Masterminds have been around since the dawn of mankind. The founding fathers of the United States were a mastermind group. Jesus and his disciples were a mastermind. King Arthur and the Knights of the Round Table were a mastermind. A little league baseball team with a coach is a mastermind. You'll find them in all areas of life, from sports to medicine to literature to politics to big business.

But few people seem to agree on the definition of a mastermind. In a private e-mail to Joe Vitale, Bill

Harris, president of Centerpointe (see Chapter 15 for details) and author of *Thresholds of the Brain,* wrote:

> My pet peeve about mastermind groups is all of the groups that say they are mastermind groups but really aren't. A real mastermind group is a group of people with the same goal, such as a board of directors or a management team. A bunch of people in different businesses who get together to help each other are NOT a mastermind group (unless they are creating an industry group with the same goal). These groups might be helpful, and perhaps you could call them co-mentoring groups or something like that, but they aren't true mastermind groups where each person has the same outcome in mind and is on the same team.

In other words, a group of people may meet at breakfast, lunch, or dinner, but that doesn't mean the group is a mastermind. They may simply be a support group, which could be one aspect of a fully operating mastermind.

But what is an authentic mastermind group?

Napoleon Hill Was Wrong

In his classic book *The Law of Success,* Napoleon Hill defined a mastermind alliance as "two or more minds working actively together in perfect harmony toward a common definite object."

There's much more to it than that simple quote, but that's a good start.

Hill considered a mastermind group to be one of the keys to success. But Hill didn't originate the idea. It's too bad that some people credit Hill for the idea, as they then dismiss the entire history of the world, with all of its numerous mastermind success stories.

Others believe that the mastermind alliance originated with Hill's mentor, the famous tycoon Andrew Carnegie. But mastermind groups were around long before then.

Carnegie, who rose from a poor Scottish immigrant boy to the richest man in the world, discovered the power of the mastermind as a young messenger boy for a telegraph service in Pittsburgh.

Escaping a life of drudgery in factories, he was offered a job with the O'Reilly Telegraph Company in 1849. The job put Carnegie in a position to see first-hand the behind-the-scenes dealings of merchants, manufacturers, bankers, and other businessmen.

In short order, young Andrew knew as much about the commercial affairs in Pittsburgh as anybody. Because of the messages that passed through his hands, he knew everybody's financial dealings, partnerships, and business plans. He also knew the credit ratings, orders for goods and services, and prices and terms for every major business in the city.

By the age of 17, Carnegie had his business education and had discovered the power of alliances in business. Throughout his rise to the top, he surrounded himself with people who knew more than he did.

Many claim that the first mastermind group was Chicago's "Big 6": Carnegie, William Wrigley Jr. (the founder of Wrigley Chewing Gum), John R. Thompson (owner of a chain of lunch rooms), Albert Lasker (owner of the Lord & Thomas ad agency, then the largest ad agency in the world), Mr. McCullough (owner of the Parmalee Express Company), and William (John Hertz) Hertz and Mr. William C. Ritchie (the owners of the Yellow Cab Company).

This group was formed in the 1920s. At the time, their combined annual income was estimated to be $25 million. In today's dollars, that's about $269 million per year! Not one of these gentlemen had an advanced education or financial advantages. All were self-made men who made their fortunes without having initial capital or extensive credit.

With the exception of the two owners of Yellow Cab, none of the six was involved in a legal partnership. They formed the group solely to get feedback for their ideas. Occasionally, they helped each other secure capital if needed on an emergency basis.

Carnegie also considered his business management team to be a mastermind group.

But this was far from Carnegie's first mastermind group.

Even as a young boy, Carnegie had a mastermind group. He organized four of his friends into the Webster Literary Society to debate the issues of the day. In the 1850s he formed a new group, called the

Original Six, who became not only a mastermind group but Carnegie's companions on trips to Europe.

Later, after moving to New York, he joined salons where he further developed his education and personal and business networks.

But the idea of a mastermind alliance goes back hundreds, even thousands of years. World leaders have had groups of advisors going back to the time of Alexander the Great. You could say Socrates' Academy and Jesus' disciples were mastermind groups. When you take into consideration ancient history, it's nearly impossible to credit any one person with creating the idea of a mastermind.

Clearly, Napoleon Hill and Andrew Carnegie didn't originate the idea, though both helped promote it.

Even the founding fathers were a mastermind.

The Junto

Ben Franklin, for example, liked to mix his civic life with his social one, and he merrily leveraged both to further his business life. This approach was displayed when he formed a club of young workingmen in the fall of 1727. It was commonly called the Leather Apron Club and officially dubbed the Junto. Franklin's small club was composed of enterprising tradesmen and artisans rather than the social elite, who had their own, fancier gentlemen's clubs. Everyone in it helped each other succeed.

Meeting one night a week, these young men discussed the topics of the day. They recommended books, shopkeepers, and friends to each other. They fostered self-improvement through discussions on topics related to philosophy, morals, economics, and politics. The group lasted for 40 years. They eventually became the American Philosophical Society.

Franklin described the Junto this way in his *Autobiography:*

> I should have mentioned before, that, in the autumn of the preceding year [1727], I had formed most of my ingenious acquaintance into a club of mutual improvement, which we called the JUNTO; we met on Friday evenings. The rules that I drew up required that every member, in his turn, should produce one or more queries on any point of Morals, Politics, or Natural Philosophy [physics], to be discuss'd by the company; and once in three months produce and read an essay of his own writing, on any subject he pleased. Our debates were to be under the direction of a president, and to be conducted in the sincere spirit of inquiry after truth, without fondness for dispute or desire of victory; and to prevent warmth, all expressions of positive opinions, or direct contradiction, were after some time made contraband, and prohibited under small pecuniary penalties.

The results of the original Junto are still evident today. The Junto gave us our first library, volunteer fire departments, the first public hospital, police departments, paved streets, and the University of

Pennsylvania. They recommended books, shopkeepers, and friends to each other. They fostered self-improvement through discussions on topics related to philosophy, morals, economics, and politics.

P.T. Barnum and the Cary Salon

In Joe's book on P.T. Barnum, titled *There's a Customer Born Every Minute,* he explains that even the great showman went to a mastermind group: "Barnum often attended the 'Cary Salon,' where he met John Greenleaf Whittier, Horace Greeley, Susan B. Anthony, and many other famous intellectuals, writers, editors, celebrities, clergymen and literary figures of his day. Alice and Phoebe Cary, American poet sisters, wrote popular poetry and attracted famous people. Barnum's choice to be part of the group's Sunday evening informal meetings helped him when it came time for networking. As a result, he had a larger circle of friends to call on when he needed help."

This, of course, was also a mastermind group, where people shared and grew from their exchanges.

Masterminds have been created for literary and political purposes as well. For example, on October 16, 1885, approximately 50 gentlemen interested in the formation of a new social club, to be located in the Back Bay district of Boston, met at the Hotel Vendome. As a result of this meeting, those present agreed to associate themselves and organize a new club. A series of organizational meetings followed, presided over by General Augustus P. Martin, at which the name Algonquin Club was chosen.

The Metaphysical Group

In 1872, an informal group of mental giants began meeting. There was Oliver Wendell Holmes Jr. (the legendary legal mind of his time), William James (the father of modern psychology), and Charles Sanders Peirce (scientist and founder of semiotics). They met for nine months and called themselves the Metaphysical Club. Their mastermind group had the purpose of exploring ideas, which they did to such historic debt that a book has been written about them, *The Metaphysical Club,* by Louis Menand.

The World's Largest Mastermind Group?

Perhaps the largest mastermind group in existence has more than 1.2 million members in the United States and more than 2 million worldwide. It's an organization that was founded by two men, Bill Wilson and Dr. Bob Watson, in Akron, Ohio, in 1935.

The organization consists of more than 105,000 groups, including 2,562 groups in correctional facilities in the United States and Canada. Can you guess which organization we're referring to?

It's Alcoholics Anonymous.

Alcoholics Anonymous a mastermind group?

Yes, absolutely.

If you're familiar with AA or similar groups, such as Narcotics Anonymous, Overeaters Anonymous, Gamblers Anonymous, or AlaNon, you've probably heard them referred to as 12-step programs. That's because there are a set of 12 guidelines all members must adhere to.

At the beginning of every AA meeting, a brief statement is read. The last line of that statement is "Alcoholics Anonymous is a fellowship of men and women who share their experience, strength and hope with each other that they may solve their common problem and help others to recover from alcoholism.... Our primary purpose is to stay sober and help other alcoholics to achieve sobriety."

Alcoholics Anonymous certainly sounds like a group of people working in harmony toward a common goal, doesn't it?

Members in AA usually meet in local groups that range from as few as four or five in some areas to several hundred in metropolitan areas. Each AA group gets together once or twice a week (or more) in churches, meeting rooms, or members' homes to share their stories about how they drank, how they came to discover AA, and how the program has helped them.

Until AA was formed, alcoholics had little chance of recovery. There was no effective treatment. Yet since its formation, millions of alcoholics have gotten sober and stayed sober simply by meeting regularly and following the guidelines established by group members.

The secret to their success seems to be the fact that an alcoholic who no longer drinks has an inherent ability to communicate and bond with a practicing alcoholic simply by sharing his or her story.

Although AA was founded in 1935, Bill Wilson and Dr. Watson took many of their ideas from another mastermind, known as the Oxford Group, which was formed in 1919. Many of the Oxford Group's ideas influenced Bill Wilson's 12 steps.

OTHER MASTERMIND GROUPS

Modern speakers and leaders know the value of mastermind groups, too. For example:

- Tom Peters, the current management guru, in his book *In Search of Excellence,* uses the term "skunkworks" to describe essentially the idea of a mastermind. A small group of people get together to work on a project and the results are usually greater than the sum of the parts. The name skunkworks was taken from the moonshine factory in Al Capp's comic strip, *Lil' Abner.*

- Zig Ziglar (leading sales trainer and motivational speaker) has an appropriate saying: "You can get everything in life you want, if you'll just help enough other people get what they want." By working together with others, as in a mastermind, you can accomplish much more.

- NBA coach Pat Riley says, "Teamwork is the essence of life. Great teamwork is the only way to reach our ultimate moments, to create the breakthroughs that define our careers, to fulfill our lives with a sense of lasting significance." A mastermind is, of course, a team.

Napoleon Hill believed that you could examine any outstanding success in business, finance, industry, or other profession and without fail find that behind the success is an individual who formed a mastermind group.

Power consists in one's capacity to link his will with the purpose of others, to lead by reason and a gift of cooperation.

—*Woodrow Wilson*

THE WISDOM OF GROUPS

In a mastermind group, the agenda belongs to the group, but each person's participation is key. Your peers give you feedback, help you brainstorm new possibilities, and set up an accountability system that keeps you focused and on track. You create a community of supportive colleagues who will brainstorm with you to move the group to new heights.

You gain tremendous insights, which can help improve your business and personal life. In a real way, your mastermind group is like having an objective board of directors.

Mastermind groups share the basic philosophy that more can be accomplished in less time by working together. Individuals meet in an open, supportive environment on a regular basis to share thoughts, ideas, opinions, and information.

James Surowiecki, in his book *The Wisdom of Crowds,* points out that a group has a larger intelligence than an individual: "If you can assemble a diverse group of people who possess varying degrees of knowledge and insight, you're better off entrusting it with major decisions rather than leaving them in the hands of one or two people, no matter how smart those people are."

As individuals, we have the ability to see things from our own perspective, our own worldview. By adding others to the mix, the group has a greater ability to share a combined intellect to see things from a new and different perspective, what some call "the third mind."

It is this collective third mind that processes information down to its essence, and it is there that thoughts crystallize into ideas. It is also where the "Aha!" moment occurs. As individuals, we cannot achieve this on our own because our myopic view can cloud our perspective. As a group with a more objective view of the world, the possibilities for expansive thinking are endless.

Obviously, there is real power in forming and being in a mastermind. Let's explore what it is a little deeper.

A REPORTER INVESTIGATES MASTERMINDS

Several people on the Internet, and some local friends, know that the authors of this book are in a mastermind group. They are naturally curious. What is a mastermind? What do you do there? Why do you do it?

Recently, a local reporter came by to celebrate Joe's birthday. She asked about masterminds. Here's part of their conversation.

"A mastermind is a group of people, usually about six in number, and usually in noncompeting businesses. They meet to help each other achieve their goals."

"Who invented it?"

"Andrew Carnegie, the famous tycoon, told Napoleon Hill about them, and Hill spread the word with a brief mention in his famous book, *Think and Grow Rich.* But masterminds go all the way back to ancient Greece. You could say Socrates had a mastermind. Or Jesus."

"What goes on in one? Is it business or spiritual or what?"

"It's a combination," Joe explained. "On one level it's an obvious support group. Each person brings their own skill set, background, business experience to the table, and everyone learns from another's perspective."

"But from a Carl Jung perspective, you also create and tap into a larger mind, a type of third mind that is formed by a meeting of supportive people."

"But what goes on?"

"The mastermind is run by whoever is the designated driver, so to speak. Basically, each person gets a chance to state their goals, their needs, and so forth. They can be designed to operate in various ways."

"How often do they meet?"

"Our group meets every Thursday, in person, at a restaurant. But I've been in two that were done entirely over the phone. And these days you could do them over the Internet with a webcam."

"Can you help me set up a mastermind?"

"That's why we're writing this book."

A MASTERMIND GROUP CAN HELP YOU REACH ANY GOAL

Mastermind groups aren't just for business. You can form a mastermind group for any goal you wish to accomplish.

Are you trying to raise money for a particular cause? Form a mastermind group.

Want to exercise more and eat right? Form a mastermind group and you'll accomplish far more than you would on your own and have a built-in support group. Joe joined a mastermind for weight loss and lost 80 pounds. He went from being the Buddha of the Internet to the Charles Atlas of the Internet.

You could even form a mastermind group to plan your next vacation. The group could help you find a good travel agent, decide on a destination, and negotiate for better travel deals using their collective purchasing power. With five to six couples, you could enjoy the benefits of a group tour without having to travel with a group of strangers.

What about remodeling your home? You could form a mastermind group in your neighborhood with four or five other couples seeking to do the same. You could share resources, tools, and materials.

Think about it. One person may be good at painting, while another has plumbing skills. One or two members might be good at planning and organization, while others are tasteful decorators. And others might be good with carpentry. You could work together on each other's projects, have fun in the process, and save a ton of money. Or, if you're not the do-it-yourself type, you can form a group to find and hire the best contractors using the group's collective buying power to negotiate better deals.

We're just skimming the surface here, but do you see the possibilities to be found in forming a mastermind group?

In the space below, write some ideas you've gained from this chapter and what types of masterminds you might want to begin:

[space left intentionally blank in the original book]

2

CASE STUDIES INSIDE THREE MASTERMIND GROUPS

Seek the counsel of [those] who will tell you the truth about yourself, even if it hurts you to hear it. Mere commendation will not bring the improvement you need.

—*Napoleon Hill*

THE HOUSTON GROUP

I (Bill) discovered the concept of a mastermind group from authors Barbara Sher and Annie Gotlieb in their book *Teamworks.* They used the term "success team" rather than mastermind, but the premise was the same.

In 1994, I was publishing a music industry directory in Houston, Texas. In the 1980s, I'd been a road manager for touring rock bands like Humble Pie and longed to return to that life. Houston offered very little opportunity to return to touring. I needed help.

I formed my first mastermind group with four other local music industry types. Pat O'Bryan owned a recording studio and was a musician. Max Shuldberg played drums for The Hunger. Joe Gavito played guitar for The Franchise and was a studio musician. Roger Igo was the sax player and manager of Global Village, a local funk band. The five of us metoncea week in the conference room of the executive suite where Pat and I shared an office.

We started our first meeting by giving a bit of background on ourselves and stating our goals. I can still clearly remember those early goals.

Pat wanted to relocate his recording studio to the Texas Hill Country. He spoke of Wimberley, a town I'd never heard of. He called it "the magic valley" and felt it would be a huge upgrade over Houston. Pat was making a good living in Houston but was frustrated by his clients. I think he yearned to spend more time on his own music and less time working on other people's albums.

Max's goal was to get a major label recording contract. The Hunger was already very successful in the Houston area. The band had some label interest but nothing concrete. They were also seeking a new manager because their current management team lacked the connections and savvy to take them to the next level.

Joe had been a professional musician since we'd first met in the mid-'70s. An excellent guitar player, drummer, and songwriter, Joe, who'd worked for years as a sideman, was considering stepping into the spotlight by forming his own group. But he was newly married and wasn't sure if he really wanted to stay in music professionally. He was considering going to electronics school and getting out of music altogether. His goal was to get clarity on what he wanted to do.

Like The Hunger, Roger Igo's band, Global Village, was quite successful on the local level. However, they weren't getting any attention outside of Texas. They were a large group, with eight or nine members. Personality conflicts were threatening to break up the group, and Roger was under a lot of pressure from his fellow band members. His goal was to determine what he should do next: step down as manager or even leave the group entirely.

My goal was to return to touring on a national or international level. I wasn't sure if I wanted to stay on the road for the rest of my life, but I wanted to at least tour Europe and see a bit more of the world before it was too late. Ideally, I wanted to work with an established band with a record deal that was touring at the club and small theater level.

I don't recall when in 1994 we originally formed the group, but by February of 1995, I was working as tour manager for Glenn Hughes. Glenn was the former bass player and singer for the band Deep Purple (and later Black Sabbath).

In less than six months, I became Glenn's manager. Before the end of 1995, I'd toured Japan, Germany, England, France, Spain, Switzerland, Austria, Belgium, Italy, and Holland. Over the next three years, I toured the world several times, working on three albums with Glenn as well as albums by other artists.

Max Shuldberg's band, The Hunger, was the first band signed by the newly formed Universal Music (formerly MCA Records). In 1996, they had a big radio hit called "Vanishing Cream" and toured as the opening act for Kiss on their huge 1996 Farewell Tour. Max continued to play with The Hunger until 2003.

Pat O'Bryan moved his recording studio to Wimberley, Texas. He has gone on to release four of his own albums. He's built quite a following in Europe and tours there once or twice a year, performing in clubs and at festivals.

Joe Gavito finished electronics school and went to work as a computer systems engineer for Exxon. He left music behind for a few years and started a family. Recently, he's returned to the music biz and owns his own recording studio. He's in much demand as a sideman and just returned from his first tour of China.

Roger Igo left Global Village and eventually the music business. Although he didn't know what his next step would be, Roger decided being a rock star wasn't what he wanted. He struggled for a few years but eventually became a successful home builder and realtor. Roger also met the love of his life, Angela, and they were married in 2001.

Each member of the group accomplished his individual goals. When I stated my goal of touring the world, I had no idea how this would come about. It seemed pretty far-fetched at the time. Even though the mastermind group wasn't directly responsible for my new position, I don't know if I would have reached those goals without their support.

I think you'll agree that both Max and Pat reached their goals as well. Although Joe and Roger didn't rise to the top of the music industry, that wasn't necessarily what they were after. Both sought clarity and were able to make their decisions with the help and support of the mastermind group. And both found success elsewhere.

And Pat O'Bryan's story doesn't end here. Later on, you'll read about the spectacular success he's enjoyed since joining my latest mastermind group.

THE AUSTIN GROUP

In early 2002, I moved to Wimberley with the intention of making my living online. I'd visited Pat O'Bryan several times since he'd moved there. After dealing with the traffic and air pollution in Houston and LA for years, I was ready for a change.

As soon as I settled in, I began what you might call Internet marketing boot camp. I studied every course, ebook, audio, and video I could find.

Prior to leaving Houston, I'd heard Joe Vitale had moved to Wimberley and planned to look him up when I got there. Although we'd never met, we'd swapped e-mails when Joe lived in Houston.

Joe and I began to meet for lunch every now and then in Wimberley. He often brought his soul mate, Nerissa Oden, along. I was a newbie marketer and didn't want to impose on Joe's time, but it was nice to have people I could meet locally to talk web marketing.

I networked in online forums, but that didn't offer the immediacy and effectiveness of my old mastermind group. I also attended several Internet marketing seminars. One of the many benefits of attending live events is the opportunity to network face-to-face. When you make your living online, face-to-face encounters are rare. My customers and joint venture partners are scattered all over the world. At live events, I was able to meet some of these people in the flesh. Interacting with people at seminars is nice, but it's not the same as participating in a regular mastermind.

I decided that it was time to form a new mastermind group. Wimberley is small, so I decided to try Austin, about 40 miles away. I contacted a few people I knew in and around Austin and posted messages on online forums seeking members.

Several people expressed interest, so I set up an initial get-together in a coffee shop. Unfortunately, there were a number of no-shows and last-minute cancellations.

Besides me, we had two newbies wanting to develop an info product online, but neither had settled on a topic. There was also a web site designer/journalist who wasn't sure if she wanted to join the group. Along with this core group, we had a few that showed up only occasionally.

The Austin group lasted for only a couple of months before I pulled the plug. The group never really clicked and attendance was inconsistent. The other problem was our meeting location. We were meeting in coffee houses. The lack of a private space led to frequent interruptions along with a too casual atmosphere. Members would arrive late, interrupting the discussion while everyone said hello, and then off they'd go to order a coffee before rejoining the group. It became more of a casual networking group than a true mastermind group. That wasn't what I was seeking, especially when I was driving 40 miles each way to attend the meeting.

So I left, and the group quickly disbanded. I had plans for a new group that would be a true mastermind.

THE WIMBERLEY GROUP

Since moving to Wimberley, I got together regularly with my old friend Pat O'Bryan, who'd been a member of my Houston mastermind group. Pat was still doing music and sometimes sought my advice about what career moves he should make. He'd also taken up painting and sold some of his artwork on eBay. Pat also got to hear all about my Internet marketing business.

One of the things Pat needed help with was publicity. I suggested he hook up with Joe Vitale. Among other things, Joe is an excellent publicist. I knew that Joe was also an amateur guitar and harmonica player.

It occurred to me that perhaps Pat and Joe could help each other, so I introduced them.

The two hit it off right away. Joe agreed to show Pat how to write press releases in exchange for guitar lessons. Also, Joe lent Pat a set of CDs introducing him to a new type of technology called binaural audio. Pat quickly saw the potential and approached Joe with an idea for a joint venture.

They agreed to form a partnership, which has gone on to produce a number of best-selling products (see www.MilagroResearchInstitute.com for details). But I'm getting a little ahead of myself.

At the time, Joe was planning a live seminar, the Spiritual Marketing Summit, to be held in Austin in January 2004. Joe invited Pat and me to attend as his guests. He also suggested that Pat release his new audio products at the seminar as a market test. The products were a big hit with the attendees, and Pat was now officially an Internet marketer.

On the drive home from the seminar, I invited Pat to join my new mastermind group. Nerissa Oden, who'd been a member of the Austin Group, let me know that Joe would join if we met in Wimberley. Pat, Joe, Nerissa, and I made four, but we needed more members.

At Joe's seminar, I met Craig Perrine. Craig was another person I'd swapped a couple of e-mails with and seen in online forums. I discovered he lived in Round Rock, just outside of Austin, and invited him to join our new group. He quickly agreed.

At the same seminar, Cindy Cashman was one of the speakers. Cindy had published several books, including *Everything Men Know about Women,* a hugely best-selling novelty book whose pages were blank. Cindy worked hard to get her book placed in nontraditional book-selling outlets, like department stores and boutiques, and women bought copies as gifts for all their friends. Although Cindy wasn't a member from day one, she's become a big part of the group.

Nerissa and Joe invited Jillian Coleman Wheeler. I'd met Jill at one of Joe and Nerissa's parties and discovered she was an expert at writing grant proposals.

So our new group was born. Other members have come and gone since we began, but the six of us have remained the core group. We've been meeting now for two years.

The benefits from this group have been tremendous. I've seen my income more than triple since forming the group. Having the group's support, advice, and cooperation has been extremely beneficial. I've done several lucrative joint ventures with group members, too, including the book you now hold in your hands.

I've also found the group members to be great accountability partners. If I announce to the group that I plan to finish a particular task by the next meeting, I know that if I fail to meet the deadline, I'll hear about it. They really help keep me on track.

Another benefit that's especially important to me is the opportunity to hang out with a group of friends who have a clear understanding of what I do for a living. Most people I meet don't understand exactly what an Internet marketer does. The business telephone directory in Wimberley lists my number under "Internet Marketing." Yet I get calls from people all the time telling me their computer has crashed and wondering how much I'd charge to come over and fix it. I also get calls from people wanting to know how much I charge per month for Internet access. So it's really a blessing to have a group that gets it.

I asked each member of our group to comment on what the mastermind group has meant to them personally:

Joe Vitale (http://www.MrFire.com)

There's magic in any group of supportive people. I love the people in our mastermind. They support, encourage, and expand on my ideas. What begins as a question, a seed, or an inkling of a plan blossoms into an exhilarating strategy, product, or entire campaign. I also love giving my own advice and input to people and watching their eyes come alive as they see new possibilities. I've created new products, coauthored new ebooks, and even orchestrated the most profitable and global event of my life with www.HypnoticMarketingStrategy.com, all as a direct result of being in this mastermind. On top of all that, the title for one of my books came out of a mastermind meeting, and it turned out to be a zinger that helped it become a best seller: *The Attractor Factor.*

Pat O'Bryan (http://www.PatOBryan.com)

"Take it to the group" has become the answer. What's the question? It could be a marketing question, a list-building question, a technical question, a copywriting question, or a question about keeping actions aligned with beliefs. The power of the mastermind, especially with minds like the ones in our group, is amazing. I credit the group with drastically increasing my income and productivity, as well as being the support and catalyst for my spiritual work.

Nerissa Oden (http://www.TheVideoQueen.com)

I'd never heard of a mastermind group. But when one was presented to me with the opportunity to join, I jumped at the chance. I even commuted for two hours every week to participate in it. And believe me when I tell you—I HATE commuting. But I did it. I did it because I wanted camaraderie, support, and guidance from as many people as possible who are like me. People wanting to make their living online.

Before the mastermind opportunity came to me, I had already turned my back on my first career and I was looking to carve out a money-making venture in the online marketplace. But that's all I knew I wanted. I didn't know how I was going to make money yet. To be honest, in the beginning I only knew how to send and receive e-mail. I didn't know how web pages and domain names worked. But I learned over time while setting up and running my first online business.

After the first year I was about to give up completely. I had already submitted to some defeating thoughts when I got part-time work at a local copy shop, which I hated myself for doing. It wasn't long after that when I began to realize that I believed life was all about working hard for someone else and making little in return. Whew!—I think I was an emotional mess back then. After my awakening, I started the hard work of reprogramming my belief system and continued my web adventures.

Then the opportunity to join the group came. And after joining I grew inspired, motivated, and more focused. I realized I had to follow my passion in order to survive the struggle periods and to eventually become and remain successful. The group's combined experience with Internet business and marketing was a welcome resource. Hearing familiar stories of isolation and struggle like mine were inherently confirming and supportive. Over time I wrote two ebooks, became a paid consultant, and developed a couple of video resource web sites. My mastermind group gave me guidance and support when I needed it. There is no other resource like it in the entrepreneur's world.

Craig Perrine (http://www.maverickmarketer. com)

The consistent input from the other members and the ongoing opportunity for me to contribute and help others has the effect of constantly benefiting me. I get great input, and I learn when I contribute (I'm often surprised by what I say).

I've had ideas that were axed in the group and good ideas that were encouraged. That's saved me the trial-and-error time I would've struggled with otherwise. Also, I've created content and have product ideas in the works with members of the group, which means my info product inventory is in good shape. I've just completed my largest product to date, a massive 30-disc home study course with three phonebook-size manuals. My mastermind group helped proofread the content and provided time and resources and even contributed content.

Clearly, this is a beneficial relationship for me, and I like to think that I have contributed to the group as well. I've come to feel that this group is not only a fantastic source of friendship and social activity among the rare people who understand what I do for a living, but also a gold mine of profitable ideas and timely opportunities that helps me boost the bottom line directly.

You can't put a price on that kind of dynamic and that kind of shared resource, and you sure don't know what you're missing if you don't have a mastermind group of your own. Let me end by saying this: For 15 years I was a loner. And though

I was successful by most standards, once I got past the steep beginner's learning curve and started to partner up with other people my success level exploded. I credit this mastermind with a great deal of that success and inspiration.

Jillian Coleman Wheeler (http://www.GrantMeR ich.com)

The best thing for me has been the group's assistance in focusing my energy. By making the mastermind meeting time a priority and being accountable to discuss my progress, I have been more consistent in committing time and energy to my business projects.

I've also benefited from the tremendous amount of information available from other members. We all bring to the table different experiences related to joint ventures, vendors, marketing, and types of projects, so we offer lots of practical support.

Finally, there's a sort of "magic" whereby the collective creativity of the whole group is greater than the sum of our individual psyches. Every one of our members, and certainly I, have experienced enormous bursts of creativity since we began to meet. We're all turning out new and interesting projects.

I have been in four different mastermind groups since 1991. I cannot put a price on what it's worth to be in good groups because it's priceless. The biggest thing being in a mastermind group has helped me with is that they're able to see things that I could not see because I was too close to my own projects.

It helps to have the group's opinions, which often means a better product for the customer.

Cindy Cashman www.CindyCashman.com)

I just recently had a mastermind meeting with five people using Skype (an online telephone service). I was talking to a friend of mine, Mark, who is a rocket scientist, and I mentioned one of the projects I was doing and he suggested getting five people together to have a meeting using Skype because we are in different states. Within a week we had our meeting and I got over two pages of ideas on possibilities for my project.

Like Napoleon Hill says in his book *Think and Grow Rich:* "No two minds ever come together without, thereby, creating a third, invisible intangible force which may be likened to a third mind."

What I have found is that the right group becomes more than just business friends. They become friends. I have shared things with the Wimberley Group (Bill, Joe, Craig, Pat, Nerissa, and Jillian) that no one else knows. I appreciate them all very much.

Thank you, Bill and Joe, for asking me to be a part of your mastermind group, and the rest of the group for your ideas, love, and support.

3

A PEEK INSIDE A MASTERMIND

None of us is as smart as all of us.

—Ken Blanchard

By now you're probably curious about how a mastermind meeting actually works. We can't give you an actual transcript of one of ours without violating everyone's privacy, but we can give you a fictional one. The following will give you a sense of how a meeting operates.

This particular meeting takes place in person, at a back room in a restaurant. Meetings can be held over the phone or over the Internet, of course. You'll learn about those later. For now, let's peek inside this live mastermind.

At noon everyone shows up at the meeting room. It would be ideal if everyone was on time, but that rarely happens. Still, to honor the group and everyone in it, this mastermind has agreed to start promptly at 12:30. This leaves 30 minutes for socializing, ordering something to eat, and getting their notes in order.

There are five people in this group, which is a good number. Too many people and the group may be too large to give everyone equal time.

The facilitator of the group can begin or ask who wants to go first. Members have agreed to state their case and ask for what they want within 15 minutes. By having a designated amount of time allotted, everyone has focus. Rarely do people go over their 15 minutes. To keep the group on track, a clock is sitting in the middle of the table, which everyone can keep an eye on.

The first person begins. In this case, it is a man who owns a buffalo ranch. Here's what he says: "I've had an interesting week. It hasn't rained in months, and my animals need water to stay healthy. We're trucking it in, but it would help if you would all pray or petition the skies or do a rain dance."

The group smiles as the rancher goes on.

"I need to drum up more business and am looking for ideas on how to market my bison. I'm making new business cards and I finally have a web site, but nothing much seems to be happening."

The rancher goes on for a few more minutes, explaining his business and what he needs. He says a few personal things about his family and challenges there, but his real focus is obviously on his business. Finally, he invites feedback.

One woman in the group used to work for a large advertising agency and today writes sales materials for clients. She suggests the following: "Have you thought about having a contest to get more business?"

The rancher says no.

"Well, you could do any number of things. You might have a guess-the-weight-of-the-buffalo contest and the winner gets a supply of meat. Or you might have a simple drawing where people buy tickets and later a number is drawn. The winner gets bison."

"But I don't know anything about the legalities of running a contest. Surely there are laws around it."

Another person in the group runs a dry cleaning store. He pipes in and says, "I have a client who is an attorney. I can ask him if he knows or if he knows anyone who can help. I can get you his business card if you like."

The rancher listens as others in the group give him ideas. He takes notes, writes down leads, and more. When his 15 minutes are up, he thanks the group.

The next person who wants to speak goes for her 15 minutes. She begins: "I'm working on a novel. It's going well, but sometimes I wonder what I'm doing. Shouldn't I just quit and get a real job? I have bills and there's no guarantee of success. I would be wasting my time. And trying to write with self-doubt in my head is a form of torture."

She continues for a few minutes, obviously spending her time complaining. Masterminds work best when people ask for help. One of the books people use as a type of manual is Joe's *The Attractor*

Factor: Five Easy Steps for Creating Wealth (or Anything Else) from the Inside Out. In that book the first step is to state what you don't want. That's what this woman has been doing. But she needs to move to Step 2: Declare what you do want. The facilitator of this mastermind interrupts to offer some help: "We're hearing about what you don't want. What is it that you want, that maybe we can help you with?"

The aspiring novelist pauses, reflects, and says, "I want to write my novel without worry or interruption."

"Could you state it in a positive way?"

"I want to write my novel with pleasure and focus, get it done as fast as possible, and find a publisher for it."

Everyone feels the shift in group energy as the novelist speaks her goal. Another person in the group has a suggestion: "I've heard that writers set a designated time to write. It might be in the morning, or late at night. Find that for yourself and then honor it. You can also set a designated time to worry. Tell yourself it's okay to have concerns, but you can have them at 3P.M."

Everyone smiles, but they all get the point, including the novelist: She has control. She has to remain disciplined while pursuing her goal. But before her 15 minutes are up, the buffalo rancher has a surprising suggestion for her: "I never told anyone, but I have a cousin who is a novelist. He's got a couple books published. I've never read them because I have bison crap to shovel, but I can get you his number. Maybe he has an agent."

The novelist beams and quickly says, "Yes! I'd pay for that information. Well, if I had any money."

"It's on the house," says the rancher.

The exchange of information in mastermind groups is free. People in them are there to help each other. Of course, if a group member wants to buy a product or service from another group member, he or she might get a friendly discount. But information is openly exchanged as a way to support each other.

Another member is ready to talk: "I'm trying to lose weight," he says. Although a mastermind is usually focused on business success, sometimes group members bring in other areas that they want to have success in. It's not unusual for a member to say he or she needs help in stopping smoking, or finding a relationship, or getting fit. Again, it depends on the agreed-on structure of the group. In this fictional case, this man wants help in getting healthy.

After he speaks for a few minutes, someone in the group asks an important question: "What are you going to do by next week's meeting to achieve your goal?"

The overweight man thinks before responding: "I'll research diets today and pick one I like. By tomorrow morning I'll be on it. By next meeting I will have lost at least a pound."

Everyone responds. The clear goal sounds achievable and the man stating it sounds believable.

In mastermind meetings, it's important that members state what they are going to do by the next meeting. This gives them direction, gets group support, and keeps them accountable. It only takes a minute to state a goal. And with group feedback, the goal can be massaged into a powerful affirmation destined for success.

This fictional meeting goes on until all members have had their 15 minutes to share. At the end of the meeting, people might stay and socialize. Usually, though, people zip out the door to maintain their typically busy schedules.

Keep in mind that meetings can take various shapes. They can be dedicated to just weight loss, for example. Joe lost 80 pounds by enlisting in a mastermind group dedicated to just that. The group was called The Mental Toughness Institute for Weight Control. Obviously, it was focused on one outcome.

The group met every Wednesday at noon by phone. Fifteen people were in it. They called from around the United States, as well as from England. In this particular mastermind, a facilitator made sure the meeting started and ended on time, and she kept it moving as well.

She would call on people, ask how they were doing, and be confrontational if they were slacking off in dieting or exercising. Again, your mastermind can take any form you like. Even confrontational ones are not emotional. There's a difference between arguing and asking direct questions about goals. All masterminds are at heart supportive.

The weight loss mastermind Joe was in required payment. Not all do, of course. Again, that's your decision. The groups I've been in, such as the one in Wimberley, are free. We could charge, but that is not how we set up the group. Plus, there's no need to charge anything. We don't have any expenses. The room is free at the restaurant and members pay for their own meal.

Again, the group can be whatever you want it to be. The mastermind for weight loss was clearly focused on one thing. Although there was openness in the group (Joe's wife of 21 years died during the time he was in the group, and everyone supported his emotional recovery), the group gathered for one purpose: Lose weight.

The group Joe and I are members of in Wimberley is more open, with people stating business goals, relationship goals, health goals, and anything else they want. Again, the group can be set up to have whatever focus you want.

Groups can have 15 minutes, or more or less, per person. We all met at Joe's home for his birthday in December 2005. Because there was a party happening that day, we decided to give everyone only 5 minutes each to state their case and their need. We were all used to at least 20 minutes each, but Joe watched the clock, everyone knew the time limit, and each of us made our contribution within that 5 minutes. When you have acknowledged limits, you can stay within them.

Finally, the mastermind described in the beginning of this chapter was fabricated. It never took place. But the sense of it is exact: People from different walks of life get together and get support. Because of their various backgrounds, you never know where the next solution will come from, or what it might be. And because it is a group, there is an energy at work more powerful than an individual's.

This is the magic of a mastermind.

Now we'll explain how you can get started with one of your own.

4

GETTING STARTED

Coming together is a beginning.
Keeping together is progress.
Working together is success.

—Henry Ford

DID ANDREW CARNEGIE AND NAPOLEON HILL GET IT WRONG?

As mentioned in Chapter 1, Bill Harris, who has read Napoleon Hill's *Think and Grow Rich* nearly a hundred times, suggested to Joe that most masterminds aren't true ones because they don't have a single stated purpose.

As we pointed out earlier, neither Carnegie nor Hill invented the mastermind concept, so who's to say what a "true" mastermind is? But is having a single stated purpose essential?

When Napoleon Hill first interviewed Andrew Carnegie, he asked him the secret to his fortune. Carnegie quickly attributed his success to his mastermind group. He then went on to describe a group of over 20 men in his employ in various areas of his steel business. These men were Carnegie's management team. They had a single purpose: making and selling steel.

Andrew Carnegie's model certainly implies that a mastermind group has a single definite purpose. But what he's describing is a group of employees or a team concept like the Cabinet that advises the U.S. president. We call this type of group an *advisory board mastermind.*

THE ADVISORY BOARD MASTERMIND

The advisory board model works well for corporate teams and community and charity groups. It's also useful for celebrities, pro athletes, musicians, and movie stars—people who have a manager, agent, attorney, and financial advisor all earning a percentage of the individual's income.

But how well would this model work for a solo entrepreneur?

Let's say I want to form a mastermind group to help build my Internet marketing business. I'd need a web designer, a programmer, a copywriter, a graphic designer, and maybe two or three other specialists, such as an attorney and an accountant.

With a group where you're the boss, there could be a danger that people won't give you honest feedback for fear of losing their position. So you'd need to choose members carefully and foster a mastermind environment where everyone feels free to speak candidly.

This would be an extremely useful team to have on my side, but without compensation, why would the other members participate? With nothing in it for them, I'm unlikely to find qualified members.

Also, regardless of compensation, if any of those people wanted help meeting their own goals, they'd have to form their own mastermind in addition to participating in mine.

So the advisory board model certainly qualifies as a mastermind group but falls short in meeting individual members' needs.

If you're in business and can afford to assemble and pay your own advisory board, then by all means do so. However, not everyone will be in a position to or necessarily want to go with an advisory board mastermind. If that sounds like you, consider forming a *mutual support mastermind.*

THE MUTUAL SUPPORT MASTERMIND MODEL

What if, instead of following the advisory board mastermind model, you suggested that this group meet to help each other accomplish their individual goals? For example, the web designer might build a web site for the attorney in exchange for the attorney helping the designer incorporate her business. And the individual members could help each other brainstorm for new ideas and provide feedback for new product or service ideas.

With this type of group, the common goal is furthering each individual member's goal. During each person's turn, it's his or her mastermind group. Everyone is focused on that member's needs. At the end of that person's time, the group refocuses its attention to the next member, and so on, until all members have taken their turn.

This is the model we've used with the Wimberley Group and the model for the Houston Group mentioned in Chapter 2.

It's also interesting to note that Carnegie himself used this alternative model with his mastermind group in Chicago, the Big 6. That group had no common purpose other than furthering the individual wealth of its members.

So, is having a single stated purpose essential?

Until recently I would have answered "No, as long as basic guidelines are agreed to and followed." Now, I'm not so sure.

I was reading a story written by the late Walter Hailey, an insurance salesman who was so good he bought the insurance company he worked for. He was describing a mastermind group he had formed several years ago in Texas consisting of a group of traveling salesmen.

Hailey's group followed a format similar to what we've done in the Wimberley Group, with one exception. Hailey's members began representing the other members' products in addition to their own.

By doing so, each member expanded his reach, plus they helped each other improve their sales pitches. But they took things even further.

The group made arrangements with supermarkets and other retailers to offer free samples and give demonstrations throughout the store. As they refined their techniques at the retail level, they began to work their way up to conventions and trade shows.

In Hailey's group, everyone essentially got the same amount of help, Rather than brainstorming on individual ideas, they came up with ways to further the entire group.

Our group doesn't work that way. Some of us coauthor books together (like this one), and we do joint ventures where we'll offer each other's products to our customers and subscribers. Some of us speak at each other's seminars.

However, all of these efforts are initiated individually. We've never created a product or promoted something as a group. Some have gotten more out of being in the group than others.

I think Hailey's method is the most effective for the entire group. It would be difficult to adopt this model in the Wimberley Group without making quite a few changes because the group wasn't organized with a single purpose in mind.

The areas of expertise and experience in our group vary quite a bit, and I doubt the entire group would want to make such a change. It's certainly something I'll consider, though, if I have the need to form another group in the future. It's something I think you should consider, too.

Either of these methods can be very effective, though. Pick the one that feels right for your situation and get started today. If you ultimately prefer the advisory board model but aren't in a position to compensate potential members, try using the mutual support model. You'll still gain enormous benefits.

DETERMINING YOUR GROUP'S PURPOSE

One of the first things you should decide is what you personally hope to gain from forming a mastermind group. Be as specific as possible. Don't set vague goals like "I want to make more money" or "I want to become famous." Get specific.

What do you want?

The definition of a mastermind is that it is a group with a specific purpose. If you are just meeting and exchanging business cards, your group may be a support or networking group, but not a mastermind group.

Joe is a magician and a member of the Society of American Magicians. When the Austin, Texas, chapter of that organization wanted to put together a team to do some marketing, they included Joe. This was a group with a defined purpose. It would classify as a mastermind.

You'll need to know the specific purpose for your mastermind to put it together. The purpose will direct who you invite to be in the group, too.

There are a number of different approaches to mastermind groups. Carnegie's Big 6 intentionally didn't have members from the same or similar industries. The goal was to allow members to discuss ideas without worrying about them being taken by a competitor.

That's certainly something you need to consider when forming your group. Your mastermind group shouldn't be a place where you have to keep things under your hat. You want to be able to float ideas freely without fear they will be leaked or stolen.

Our Wimberley group is very trusting. Joe Vitale has a saying that we all like: "Worry more about creating an idea *worth* stealing than about it being stolen." In our group, we are supportive and respectful.

Another challenge with a group formed of people within the same industry is that people tend to do things the same way they've always done them. They rarely look outside their own industry for solutions. In other words, if everyone in your group is in the dry cleaning business, you're all seeing the same problems and trying the same solutions. Yet if an outsider sat in on your meetings—maybe someone who runs a movie theater—he or she would see your situation with an objective and fresh view, which could lead to surprising solutions. If you're not careful, a group of people from the same business could lead to meetings where everyone just gripes about the way things are rather than finding solutions.

And groups of people in the same industry rarely think outside the box. They hope for a magic lightbulb creative moment to solve their problems.

The reality is that quite often, for every business problem you face, there is probably a solution to be found within *another* industry.

By having a group composed of people from different industries you might easily discover effective tactics that your competitors won't be aware of.

Obviously, this isn't an issue if you've formed a mastermind group to accomplish fitness goals, discuss spiritual issues, or work on personal development. It only applies to business masterminds.

However, for business masterminds, choosing members from different industries does have drawbacks. For example, the Wimberley Group is made up entirely of Internet marketers. Though we each have different specialties, there is a lot of overlap. And sometimes there is a little concern about sharing ideas.

We're all good friends and trust each other, which is an essential element in a mastermind group. However, occasionally an idea will come up and as others jump in and expand on the idea with each member contributing, it can get a little awkward because two or three members could easily capitalize on the idea. Those who have contributed key elements may feel a little ownership. But it all works out, and we've never had any conflicts over it.

A good example is this book. We've discussed writing this book for a while but have taken a long time to write it because we've given priority to other projects. Other members of the group have been eager to either write their own book or promote ours. They've discussed our group in their individual newsletters, and their readers have responded with a lot of questions. To the group's credit, everyone has held back and waited for us to finish our book since we first came up with the idea.

But we know it's been tough on them to wait. If we were all from different industries, something like this wouldn't be an issue. On the other hand, there are tremendous advantages to having members in the same or similar industries.

In our group, we've done a number of joint ventures. There have been coauthor projects, like Joe Vitale and I creating *The Ultimate Guide to Creating Moneymaking Ebooks,* and Pat O'Bryan has done several coauthor projects with Joe, including *The Milagro Manifestation Method.* And obviously, the very book you are reading is a joint effort with Joe, too.

We've also promoted each other's products to our own customers and subscribers, which has been beneficial to everyone.

Finally, there's the shared resources aspect. We've swapped tips for web hosting services, graphic designers, shopping cart systems, software, and more. Although we haven't taken it to this level yet, I can see how we could leverage our collective buying power to get discounts on various products and services, too.

Those are the pros and cons of going with a group where all your members are in the same or competitive industries. Ultimately, it's up to you what type of group you wish to form.

SAME OR SIMILAR INDUSTRY GROUP

If you're forming a group within the same industry, consider seeking members with diverse skills or niches within the same market. For example, in our group:

- Joe Vitale is an excellent writer. He's a best-selling author and a skilled copywriter and publicist. Within Internet marketing, he tends to focus more on the self-help, motivational, and spiritual side of marketing. And Joe is very good at evaluating both ideas and sales copy.

- Craig Perrine's specialty is list building and coaching. He's very good at expanding on an idea. Whenever we have an idea for a new product, we know Craig will always come up with an idea to make it better.

- Nerissa Oden specializes in video. She's worked on major motion pictures as well as documentaries and has edited seminar videos. When we have a question about using video on our web sites or in our products, it's Nerissa we call on. Although she has less experience with marketing, that also means she takes fewer things for granted. When we get feedback from Nerissa, she usually raises the type of observations and objections my potential customers would. That's extremely valuable.

- Pat O'Bryan specializes in audio products and ebooks. A musician, record producer, and recording studio engineer, Pat knows audio far better than most web marketers. As a result, he's advanced quickly by releasing products that capitalize on his skills. Pat almost always challenges the accepted norms. So he challenges us and suggests unique approaches rather than the same old, same old.

- Jillian Coleman Wheeler's specialty is government grants and real estate. She also has a background in psychology (see Chapter 11, Jill's piece on group dynamics) and is an excellent editor. Of all the members of our group, she has the most experience dealing with the corporate world. So Jill brings yet another valuable perspective to the group.

- Cindy Cashman is an author, coach, and idea person. She was the creative genius behind *Everything Men Know about Women* (the blank book), *The Book of Smiles, Life Lessons for Women, Life Lessons for Couples,* and many other books written under various pseudonyms. Cindy is a total dynamo and very inspiring. We've seen her come into meetings with the type of idea that would take most people months, if not years, of planning and turn it into a profitable business in weeks. Just being able to observe Cindy in action is valuable, not to mention her feedback on our own ideas.

- One of Bill's specialties is the nuts and bolts of Internet marketing, things like web site automation, hosting, and web site design. He's usually the person everyone calls on when they have a technical question or want an opinion on a product or service that they're considering using. And as he reviews web sites as part of his business (Master SiteReviewer.com), he, along with Joe and Craig, are often called on to critique a member's sales copy. Joe and Craig are very good at this, too, but each often picks up on things the other doesn't.

Although there is some duplication of skills within the group, we've got a lot of diversity, too. It's a good balance. If we had six techies in the group, we'd probably spend more time arguing than making any forward progress.

So diversity is the key, whether you're going with a same industry group or a multi-industry group. Look for people from different backgrounds, of different ages, and with different personal styles. If you introduce an idea and need feedback, you want as many ideas and takes as you can get. If you choose members who are too similar, the first person will fire off some feedback and the rest will just nod their heads in agreement and you'll get little additional input.

MIXED-GENDER OR SINGLE-GENDER GROUP?

Another thing to consider is whether you want a mixed-gender or an all-male or all-female group. Remember, you need diversity. And I'm not trying to be politically correct. Men and women often have completely different ways of looking at things. Having both men and women will give you feedback you won't get in a single-gender group. Keep that in mind if you market a product or service to both men and women.

On the other hand, men and women often communicate in very different ways. This can be a source of friction for some members. If you take the time to get to know prospective members before committing to having them join the group, it will help you determine if their communication style fits your own. Be sure to read Jillian Coleman-Wheeler's chapter on group dynamics for more details on this topic.

BEFORE THE FIRST MEETING

Prior to your first meeting, we suggest surveying each person to see what his or her particular skills are. Your goal is to discover what each member will contribute and what each will gain by joining your group. For a free survey form to help with this step, go to www.MeetAndGrowRich.com.

Also, don't be afraid to approach people higher up the ladder than you are. Which person do you think you'd learn more from, a newbie or an experienced person who's already had some success? It's the latter, of course.

People are usually afraid to do this. They assume that the more experienced person won't be interested in joining their group. Don't make that mistake. You're the one going to the trouble of organizing the group, so you're making an important contribution. Plus, when you get one successful person to join, you can usually attract others.

When I (Bill) first started the Austin Group, I didn't ask Joe Vitale to join. I assumed that because I had less experience and Joe was a recognized guru, he wouldn't be interested in joining.

When the Austin Group didn't work out, Nerissa told me that if I formed a group in Wimberley, Joe would join us. As you can imagine, I was thrilled to have him. Mentioning Joe's participation helped recruit others from as far away as Austin.

And let's not forget that Joe would not have joined without seeing some benefit to his being in the group. "I needed to get out of the office more, brainstorm with others, have some social time, and see how I could support others while they supported me," Joe explained later. "I was flattered to be asked and delighted to join."

So don't exclude anyone you'd like to see in your group. You never know who might say yes.

HOW MANY MEMBERS IS BEST?

For a vacation or home remodeling mastermind, you might want to go with five or six couples. For most other types of groups, ideally, you want five to six members. When you have more, meetings can drag on too long.

If each member gets 20 minutes and you've got six members, that's two hours. Getting the meeting started, taking a short break in the middle, and wrapping things up will add a half hour. That's two and a half hours. Beyond that is too long, especially if you meet once a week. So if you choose to go with more than six members, we'd recommend limiting each person's turn to 10 or 15 minutes.

On the other hand, when you have fewer than five members, meetings are unproductive when one or two people can't make it. You'll end up either canceling meetings or having people drop out.

It's possible that you will need to start out with more members than you ultimately want. The Wimberley Group currently has 6 members, but we've had as many as 10. Over time, you'll find that one or two members have a problem with attendance. Or they'll decide the group isn't for them.

Early on, with the Wimberley Group, we had members missing two to three meetings per month. We'd have three people one week and nine the following week. Because many had been absent for weeks, meetings sometimes ran four hours because extra time was needed to get caught up.

Out of concern that our group would drift apart, we announced that we wanted to narrow the group down to six firmly committed members. We asked all members to either commit to regular attendance or let someone else have their spot. It was a bit awkward at first, but we ended up getting a strong core group with consistent attendance.

Another way to go about this initially is to just seek one other person to mastermind with. Make sure you get along well and trust this single mastermind partner. Once you're comfortable with him or her, start looking for a third member together, taking the same approach. Once you've integrated the third member and there's a spirit of trust and harmony, the three of you can begin looking for a fourth member. And you can continue this process, adding one member at a time, until you reach your ideal group size.

If you take this approach, your chances of building a strong mastermind are great, but you'll notice that each time a new member joins the group, you'll have to take a few steps backward before moving forward. That's due to the mandatory "getting to know each other phase" that all groups go through. A trio, for example, that's been meeting together for several weeks will develop a level of trust that allows them to be comfortable sharing certain information. When a new person joins the group, the older members won't feel that same level of comfort. Once everyone feels comfortable with the newest member, that level of trust will return.

QUALITIES TO LOOK FOR IN POTENTIAL MEMBERS

First and foremost, you want people who are highly motivated, are goal-oriented, and have a positive attitude. Avoid complainers and those seeking more of an emotional support group. They'll be a constant drain on the group.

And please don't think we mean to imply that a mastermind group can't be supportive. They can be; ours certainly is. But you don't want to attract people that are "stuck" and all talk and no action when it comes to making a change.

Over time, you may find that the group occasionally takes on a group therapy feel. That's natural once people get to know and trust each other. In the year that we've been together, we've all had help from the group dealing with various personal crises.

But I have had firsthand experience seeing one negative person completely disrupt a good group.

Several years ago, I was involved in an organization formed to help promote the Houston music scene. In every meeting, the members would do nothing but complain and blame others for all their problems.

There were some good people in the leadership of that group, but one member did nothing but whine.

Any suggestions made by the others were usually greeted with pessimism. This man was very angry with the realities of the music industry. Rather than adapt or improve, he preferred to play the victim and point fingers. To make matters worse, he sometimes showed up after having a few too many adult beverages.

As long as he was around, there was little harmony in the group. In the end, it took some rather extreme measures to get rid of this particular member. When we did, the group was transformed, and some very positive things happened.

So I strongly suggest you choose members carefully and invite new members on a probationary basis. If you've got one of the negative types, you'll probably know after spending a little time with him or her on the phone. If not, you'll definitely know by the time the first meeting is over. Don't invite that person back.

Look for people eager to make improvements in either their career, business, or other areas. It's okay if they haven't clearly defined their goals yet, but they shouldn't be so afraid to take action that they'll never actually do anything.

On the other hand, if you're talented but dealing with confidence issues, consider forming a group that's more supportive. Also, consider working with a therapist or a coach to deal with your more pressing personal issues. It can be difficult to mix superachievers with someone prone to procrastination. The achievers will lose patience with the procrastinator and vice versa.

Sometimes these two personality types can work together, but they can just as easily clash. It often boils down to chemistry. Some groups have it, some don't. As you can see from my own experience with the Austin Group, I didn't succeed on the first try.

I brought Nerissa from the Austin Group, Pat from my original Houston Group, and together we formed the Wimberley Group. If your first group doesn't work out, take any members you feel comfortable with, seek out a few more people, and form a new group.

We'll talk more about personality types in the next chapter.

WHERE TO FIND MEMBERS

If you're forming a mastermind for personal goals such as weight loss, pursuing a hobby, or remodeling a home, finding members isn't difficult. Start with your friends and neighbors.

If you know only one or two candidates, ask each person you contact if he or she knows anyone who would be interested in joining your group. If you can find at least one other person interested in putting a group together, it'll be a lot easier to find members. Two heads are better than one.

You can draw on people from your work, school, church, fitness club, chamber of commerce, or other organizations you belong to.

You can run a classified ad seeking members. Weekly lifestyle/entertainment papers are usually best for this. You can say you're forming a small business networking team or mastermind group.

There are a number of ways to do this online using networking web sites such as Ryze. com, Meetup. com, or Yahoo groups. As we finish this book, we're launching MeetAndGrowRich.com, a web site devoted to helping you assemble your mastermind group and seek potential members. Make this your first stop when starting a new group.

You can also do an Internet search by entering a topic like health, marketing, business, or whatever type of group you have in mind followed by the words "forum" or "group." You'll often find a number of online bulletin boards or discussion groups this way.

Here's a copy of the ad I ran in an online membership forum for my first Internet marketing mastermind:

Any Members in the Austin, TX, Area?

I'm seeking Internet marketers in the Austin/San Marcos area for a possible networking group or to just hook up to swap ideas, etc. If you're interested, please reply here in the forum or shoot me an e-mail at...

That ad yielded only one good candidate, but she in turn brought three others to the group. The downside of placing an ad is that you're dealing with total strangers.

Before meeting in person, screen potential members by phone. (To get a script to assist you in interviewing potential members, please visit MeetAndGrowRich.com.) Also, I recommend scheduling at least the first two meetings in a coffee shop, restaurant, or other public place.

For a business group, start by making a list of people you already know. Each person you speak with can lead to two or three other prospects. Always ask each person you speak with if he or she knows anyone else who might be interested in joining a mastermind.

Vendors who call on your business can be helpful here, especially if you're forming a group of people within the same industry. They may help you find good candidates in other industries, too.

Your banker, accountant, attorney, and other professionals may all be good resources. Check the business section of your local newspaper, too. Newspapers often run stories on successful local businesspeople. Why not invite one of these people to join your group?

One very good approach is to find people from completely different industries that share the same customers. For example, let's say you have a local dry cleaning business. What other services and products are your customers likely to buy locally? Let's make a list:

- Car wash/detailing service

- Carpet cleaning service
- Movie rentals
- Handyman service
- Restaurants
- Grocery stores
- Plumbers
- Moving companies
- Pizza delivery
- Hair salons
- Gyms
- Realtors

That's just 12 off the top of my head. I'm sure you could come up with an even bigger list.

Now imagine if you formed a mastermind group with half a dozen businesses on this list.

What if you wrote a letter addressed to each of your customers recommending a fellow member's carpet cleaning service? Perhaps they could offer your customers a special discount if they mention your name or use a coupon. Imagine how much more effective a promotion like that would be than if the carpet cleaner just sent a coupon in the mail.

Of course, in return, the carpet cleaner sends out a similar letter promoting your business. Each member of the group could do a similar exchange. Think of the additional income you could gain this way.

And that's just one thing you could accomplish with this type of mastermind group.

Regardless of where you find them, how many members you choose, and what type of group you wish to form, you're going to be dealing with a variety of personalities.

If you don't choose carefully or you don't have strong people skills, your chances of success could be limited. Your group can go from cooperative to unmanageable.

Would you like to learn how to avoid problems like these? We thought so. We'll show you how in the next chapter.

5

PERSONALITY TYPES

A group becomes a team when each member is sure enough of himself and his contribution to praise the skills of the others.

—Norman Shiple

A famous Internet marketer once created a mastermind of historic scope. He created a large organization and had the members break into smaller groups, so no one group had more than six members. But this same person failed to take into account personality types.

One of the members of the main mastermind, which was the first group in this organization, was very controlling. He ended up using the group to his own end, enlisting people into multilevel marketing programs. The organization crumbled because of this and other errors in judgment. Had everyone been more aware of personality types, they might have prevented this problem.

You'll want to be aware of the different personality types you'll find in any group situation, including a mastermind. Your group should be supportive, so any negative element will have to be excluded or disinvited. Let's look at some of the personality types you might encounter along the way to meeting and growing rich. The following are based on the Enneagram.

The Enneagram is one of the newest personality systems in use, and emphasizes psychological motivations. Its earliest origins are not completely clear, but many therapists and psychologists are turning to it to better understand their clients.

REFORMER

The reformer will try to produce order. He or she will focus on doing everything the right way. Of course, there is no "right way" to achieve anything. The nature of a mastermind is openness to possibilities. If there were only one way to do anything, you probably wouldn't need a mastermind.

Fear is what usually runs the belief system of a reformer. If you encounter a reformer, assure him or her that your mastermind group is one of safety and support. Reformers usually fear doing something wrong. Once it dawns on them that there is no wrong way to be in a mastermind (short of disruptions of the flow), they will relax.

HELPER

Then there's the helper. This person wants to help everyone. There's nothing wrong with that at heart, but it can lead the group astray. In other words, a helper has a need to be loved. The inherent fear is of not being liked by the group. In an attempt to be liked, or even loved, this person might try to control conversations and take extra time.

Again, assure this person—assure everyone in the group—that they are there by invitation, they are all loved and liked, and their job is to equally support each other.

MOTIVATOR

Motivators want to cheer everyone on. They are coaches or cheerleaders, at least in their own mind. They need to be admired. Their fear is rejection. In a vain attempt to win approval, they may try to dominate the group by cheering everyone on. That's not wrong, but it may cause an imbalance in the group's energy.

The way to handle motivators is to assure them that a mastermind is not a competition. No one person needs cheered on to the finish line. Every member of your group needs cheering, and everyone should offer it, to the degree they are comfortable.

ROMANTIC

Romantics are warm, perceptive, and sensitive. They seek plenty of compliments and strive to give them as well. The problem is, they may experience dark moments of isolation and loneliness. They may refer to the mastermind as therapy. Obviously, this isn't the purpose of most masterminds. (There can be self-help masterminds, of course.)

Romantics often have a fear of being defective in the eyes of others. They may turn to the group for approval. All members of your mastermind need to be treated equally and assured that they are whole and complete as they are. The group is designed to help people evolve and achieve, not to fix any flaws in personality.

THINKER

Masterminds often attract thinkers. These are the people seeking to analyze and understand the world. They secretly fear being overwhelmed by the world. As a result, they may spend more time thinking and less time doing.

All masterminds should be focused on achieving something. To do so, action usually has to be taken on some level. One good idea is to ask participants to do things each week, whether homework or self-directed action. This can help turn thinkers into balanced doers.

SKEPTIC

Skeptics have a "fortress mentality." They allow little in because they are skeptical about the world at large. They secretly fear being abandoned. Deep inside, they are very insecure.

You may not want skeptics in your group. Having a healthy dose of devil's advocate thinking is good for reasoning out the feasibility of ideas, but an outright skeptic could destroy your group's momentum. If you have someone in your group showing signs of skepticism, you might assure that person that his or her ideas are welcome. This will remove the fear of rejection and lessen the skepticism.

ENTHUSIAST

The enthusiastic group member is happy and open to new things. He or she has a need to stay happy and "up." This could also be a problem. If enthusiasts don't feel like they are exploring the world, they may become restless and unhappy. This could show up in your group as a disruption.

These people need to refrain from instantly jumping into the next project before fully experiencing the one they're in.

LEADER

Leaders are just what they appear to be. They have a desire to be strong, independent, and self-reliant. They have a fear of submitting to others. They don't want to feel like they've given their power away. In your group, you need to watch that they are balanced in leading as well as being led.

PEACEMAKER

Peacemakers seek union in the group. They are sincerely open to others and respectful of them. But they have a fear of separation. If the group appears out of harmony, they may take over the group in an attempt to make peace. These people need to realize that union in any group has an ebb and flow to it. Perfect harmony in ideas may not always be present.

None of these types is good or bad in and of itself. Your job as group leader is to simply keep a watchful eye on the personalities in your group. It's not wise to try to change anyone, but you (or the designated facilitator) can make sure the group is run in an orderly way and that the meetings proceed as intended.

6

HOW TO RUN A MASTERMIND MEETING

The greater the loyalty of the group toward the group, the greater is the motivation among the members to achieve the goals of the group, and the greater the probability that the group will achieve its goals.

—Rensis Likert

HOW OFTEN TO MEET

We've had groups that met weekly and groups that met every other week. Our preference is meeting weekly. It keeps things consistent. If you meet every other week, you spend too much time recounting what you've been up to since the previous meeting. Plus, members who miss a meeting are out of the loop for a month. That's too long.

However, we've heard of groups that meet monthly and have been quite successful. Also, you might try meeting once a week for a while and then cutting back if the group feels that schedule is too restrictive.

Another alternative is to meet weekly but alternate between an in-person meeting one week and a conference call the following week. This may be a good solution if making it to a weekly meeting is too demanding.

WHERE TO MEET

A mastermind group requires a quiet, private place where people feel comfortable sitting for two to three hours. Select a spot with room to park that's safe and convenient for everyone in the group.

With the Houston Group, I was fortunate enough to have a conference room in my office with comfortable chairs, good lighting, and access to beverages and restrooms. It was quiet and private. Check with your members to see if anyone has access to a space like this.

The Austin Group chose to meet in coffee houses. They were comfortable but were not ideal for mastermind meetings. First, they weren't private. Strangers would often be seated within earshot, and if the shop was crowded, finding seating for a group of six could be a challenge. Also, there was usually music playing in the background and it could get fairly loud.

But probably the worst part of meeting in coffee shops is that it created too casual an atmosphere for a business meeting. Members often arrived late and left early. We'd have people walking in 20 or 30 minutes late, and the meeting would stop while everyone said hello. Then the newcomers would go line up for coffee and we'd end up spending 10 minutes catching them up on what was covered before they arrived.

We also occasionally had people show up on time or a few minutes late and announce that they could stay for only a few minutes but wanted to drop by and say hello. A coffee shop makes it easy for these types of things to happen. It seems natural due to the environment. The same people wouldn't dream of doing this if you met in a conference room.

So, though a coffee shop is okay for the initial get-together when people are meeting for the first time, find a different, permanent meeting place before your second meeting.

Some mastermind groups choose to meet in members' homes. Either they meet at the same place every week or rotate, with a different member playing host each week. If you decide on this approach, make sure every member of the group is comfortable with the idea. If it's not unanimous, don't do it. Hosting five or six people for a few hours isn't everyone's cup of tea. However, if everyone feels comfortable with the idea, go for it.

If you can afford it, you can always rent time in a small conference room in a hotel or executive suite. With everyone chipping in, it isn't that expensive. You can often find free meeting space at community centers, public libraries, chamber of commerce centers, churches, and other public spaces.

If you're having difficulty finding a place, I suggest checking your local newspaper's group meeting calendar. Most newspapers or entertainment weeklies have a list of meetings for various groups in the area. Check to see where these groups are meeting. Then either contact the location or the group to see if you can use the space, too.

Where I live, there aren't a lot of meeting rooms available. The chamber of commerce has a room, but the space is booked so far in advance it's impossible to reserve it for two or three hours on a weekly basis.

Ultimately, we contacted restaurants in the area until we found one with a private room they'd let us use. The room wasn't being used at lunchtime and was perfect for our needs.

An added advantage to meeting in a restaurant is that it encourages people to arrive on time. We arrive at noon and take a few minutes to socialize and order lunch before we get started. We still occasionally have people arrive late, but our situation is a bit unusual. Two of our members drive in from as far as 50 miles away.

If you decide to go the restaurant route, I suggest finding a place that serves not only good food but a nice variety. The first restaurant we used offered a nice private room, and the food and service were good. However, it was a Mexican food restaurant, and after a couple months, everyone was tired of Tex-Mex. So we moved to the Cedar Grove Steakhouse, a place with a nice variety, healthier fare, and a private room with a view.

WHEN TO MEET

The day and time don't matter as long as both are mutually convenient. The important thing is to remain consistent. For my group, it's every Thursday at noon. Because we're all self-employed, we're free to meet during regular business hours.

If you don't have that freedom, choose an evening or weekend. When determining how long to set aside, plan on 20 minutes per member, plus about half an hour for opening and closing remarks, a short break midmeeting, and, if you're in a restaurant, time to pay the tab.

Regardless of what time you choose, always start your meetings on time. And those who arrive late should be expected to join the meeting in progress. Don't take time to stop and catch them up.

CHOOSING A LEADER

In the three mastermind groups I've worked with, I've been the leader. This usually is an unofficial outcome of my having started the group. Does it have to work that way? Not necessarily.

Being the leader is an added responsibility. I'm usually the one who has to relay messages and contact people if there's been a change. That in itself isn't really a burden, but there are other responsibilities.

If there's a problem, I'm the one that gets to play the heavy. The biggest challenge for me is keeping the meeting running on time. Some people don't like it when the meetings run too long.

There's sometimes a little tension being the timekeeper. In our group, you get 20 minutes to talk about what's on your mind and then get feedback from the rest of the group. I find that most people are comfortable getting through what they need to say within the 20 minutes. The time challenges occur when getting feedback.

The person whose turn it is usually is keeping an eye on the clock. However, the people giving feedback usually aren't. It's hard to get them to stop when time's up. They'll talk for a minute or two after time is expired, and then the person getting the feedback wants to respond. And then someone else will jump in. There's sometimes a tendency to try to solve a problem completely during the allotted time. And that's usually not going to happen in 20 minutes.

What helps to keep everyone on track is to review the rules periodically and get everyone to agree to them. And get everyone to realize that it's okay if they don't get a full round of feedback from every single person in the group.

An alternative to having a fixed leader is rotating leadership. You could, for example, designate a new leader every month. Some mastermind groups that meet in members' homes opt to have the leader be the person who's hosting the meeting.

The leader is responsible for notifying the group of any changes, keeping time, and handling any tasks related to the meeting room, such as making reservations and arranging for beverage service. The leader should be the one who calls the meeting to order and keeps everyone on track as the meeting proceeds. (For more information on leading a meeting, see Chapter 14, "10 Tips for Facilitating Mastermind Group Meetings.")

STAYING IN TOUCH BETWEEN MEETINGS

At the initial meeting, I ask members to fill out a brief form with all their contact info, including e-mail address. Our group prefers to stay in touch via e-mail.

The advantage to e-mail is that when you need to deliver a message, one e-mail does the trick. To deliver the same message by phone would require half a dozen phone calls and repeat calls when leaving a message isn't possible.

Most e-mail programs like Microsoft Outlook allow you to place e-mail addresses in groups. In Outlook, I set up a group address called "mastermind." Whenever I need to e-mail the group, I type "mastermind" in the "To" field and the message goes to the entire group. This saves typing each member's address individually.

Some people don't like e-mail and prefer the telephone. You can use whatever your group feels comfortable with.

MEETING FORMAT: THE FIRST MEETING

I've seen many creative ideas for breaking the ice at the first meeting. Quite frankly, I've never used them. In my groups we have always chosen to simply take turns introducing ourselves and giving a little background info.

Beyond that, you want to identify each member's long-term goal. If members don't have one yet, their first task is to get a long-term goal. From that first meeting and every meeting that follows, members should give themselves a homework assignment or short-term goal for the coming week. A good way to track your progress is to use a form like the one we've adopted in the Wimberley Group. We'll explain how it works at the end of this chapter.

One other thing you can do during the first meeting is name your group. This one's optional, but why not make that your group's first collective goal?

GROUND RULES

You'll want to lay down some ground rules. Here are a few suggestions.

Start meetings on time. This is true regardless of what type of group you have, but especially for business-based masterminds. The group should be treated with the same respect you'd show your best client. That means don't be late and don't skip meetings casually. When a member is late, the group should never backtrack and fill the late arrival in.

Being late cheats everyone in the group. Not only does your late arrival interrupt the meeting, but your absence means some of the members didn't get the benefit of feedback from the entire group.

It's also natural for members to want to socialize a little when they first arrive. One way to allow for that is to set aside the first 15 to 30 minutes for social time, and for ordering if you're in a restaurant. That also prevents someone's turn from being interrupted by the wait staff serving your meal or taking orders.

End meetings on time. The key here is using a timekeeper. If everyone takes an extra 5 to 10 minutes during his or her turn, that can turn a 2-hour meeting into 3 hours. Members may not complain. In fact, they may enjoy staying late. But in the future, they'll realize that with travel time, they're losing half a day every week. Absences will go up, and you'll have members dropping out.

Notify other members in advance if you have to miss the meeting. Don't leave your fellow members worrying about you. If you don't call, they may worry that you've had car trouble or been in an accident. Make sure to phone or e-mail that you can't make it and why.

Set a specific time limit for each member to speak. I recommend 20 minutes per person. Use some type of timer, whether it be a stopwatch or a kitchen timer. We use a small digital kitchen timer that looks like an hourglass. It's small enough to carry around easily and you don't have to reset it at the end of each person's turn. It's made by Polder and can be found for less than $20 at Skymall.com, Shop.com, or Hom eVisions.com.

It's important that not only the person sharing but the entire group be aware of how much time is left. I find that it's often not the person whose turn it is that eats up the clock but members giving feedback. That's because there's a tendency to want to completely solve every person's problem. And there simply isn't enough time to do that in 20 minutes.

In addition, as I said earlier, *someone needs to actually be in charge of time.* It may be tempting to ignore this suggestion. However, if you don't keep track of time, you'll find that some members will talk for 45 minutes without realizing it.

Finally, you'll need to *compare schedules and resources to determine how often, where, and when you'll meet.*

REGULAR MEETING FORMAT

For subsequent meetings, each person gets 20 minutes. It helps for group members to make out a brief checklist of things they plan to bring up during their turn. When it's your turn, you can either go through the entire list and then ask for feedback or solicit feedback for each item on your list before going on to the next item.

What you share can be personal or professional. We've had members ask for help sticking with their diet or exercise program. Others have discussed their problems trying to devote enough time to their business without neglecting their families. The important thing is for each member to feel that he or she is gaining something by participating.

In our group, some of us give ourselves homework assignments. If you tend to procrastinate, this can be a good way to keep you on track. You'll know that if you didn't finish your homework, the group will hold you accountable. For many, this is the key benefit of belonging to a mastermind group.

What kinds of things show up on members' weekly lists? Members might need feedback on a new product idea or marketing campaign. They might need to deal with a technical issue or need resources like an attorney, web designer, or accountant.

If you set a goal or gave yourself an assignment the previous week, start your list by sharing whether you took the action or reached your goal.

If you have several things on your list, I'd suggest waiting until you've covered each before asking for feedback. If not, you're likely to run out of time before getting to everything on your list.

And you don't necessarily have to ask for feedback. After speaking, you can tell the group what you need. That might be feedback or holding you accountable to reach a certain goal.

It's important that each member participate in the feedback process. If you have something to say, don't feel intimidated that other members might have more experience than you do. The idea is for each person to get feedback from a variety of perspectives.

When you do offer feedback, keep it brief and to the point. Be aware of the clock so you're not monopolizing the other person's time. If all you want to say is that you agree with what someone else has said, say that and yield to the next person.

After all members have had their turn, unless there's any group business, the meeting is adjourned.

7

LONG-DISTANCE MASTERMIND GROUPS

The only thing that will redeem mankind is cooperation.

—*Bertrand Russell*

MASTERMIND BY TELEPHONE

Although I prefer meeting in person, for a variety of reasons that's not always possible. Many successful mastermind groups meet strictly by phone. In his book *The Success Principles,* Jack Canfield mentions that his group meets every two weeks by telephone. They also meet for two days in person on a quarterly basis.

Marketing guru Dan Kennedy hosts a million-dollar mastermind that includes Internet marketing experts Derek Gehl and Yanik Silver, real estate whiz Ron Legrand, and fitness hot shot Matt Furey. They meet by phone, supplemented by annual meetings when they get together in person. Each member pays Kennedy a five-figure fee every year to belong to this exclusive group.

Telephone meetings are held via conference calls. Traditional telephone conference calling can be expensive, ranging from 4.5 cents to 15 cents per minute. I've found a way to cut these costs to a flat $100 per month for a weekly two-hour call for up to 30 people. That does not include a toll-free line, though, so there will also be long-distance charges. However, there are unlimited long-distance packages available through land lines, mobile phones, and Internet services like Roadrunner, Skype, and Vonage. If you've got half a dozen members, this works out to about $17 per month per member.

Because technology is changing so fast, rather than suggest a technology that may be outdated by the time you read this, we've set up a page on our web site where you can get the details on the most efficient and cost-effective ways to master-mind online. For details, sign up for our free master-mind kit at http://www.MeetAndGrowRich.com.

There are a number of pros and cons to meeting by phone.

Advantages

- It cuts down on people showing up late.
- It saves time and travel expenses.
- It allows you to meet with people outside your local area.
- Meetings start and end on time due to the time limit on the calls.

- There are no food or beverage costs.
- It tends to eliminate cross talking.

Disadvantages

- There are long-distance charges.
- There's no personal contact.
- There is no opportunity to demonstrate or display new products or marketing materials.

MASTERMIND ONLINE

If members are Internet savvy and properly equipped, you can choose to use a chat room with voice capability. The advantages are the same as meeting by phone but less costly.

Using a service like Yahoo Messenger along with computers with Internet access and a microphone, a group can meet any time they'd like with no costs involved. This works best when members have high-speed access. You can also add a webcam so you can see your fellow members.

The drawback is that there can be technical problems. People get knocked offline if they're using dial-up. Also, these systems tend to crash from time to time, which can be disruptive.

On the plus side, a service like Yahoo allows international participation. You'd still have restrictions due to time differences, but it's certainly possible to have a global group.

As we mentioned earlier in the book, we are putting together a new online community that will support mastermind groups. You can seek members for a local, telephone, or online group, read stories about successful masterminds around the globe, and network with other mastermind groups. You'll also be able to keep up with the latest online meeting technology. For details, go to www.MeetAndGrowRich.com.

CASE STUDY: SELF-EMPLOYED SUCCESS MASTERMIND GROUP

Karyn Greenstreet is an internationally known speaker, author, and self-employment expert. She's been forming and facilitating mastermind groups for years. Her current group meets both by telephone and online message boards. Here's the story of her current mastermind group.

Being self-employed and working from home can be a lonely experience, and though family and friends are supportive, it's not the same as connecting with a group of other self-employed people who know what it's like in the trenches.

I've been creating and running mastermind groups for 20 years around many different themes and topics, but had a profound need to belong to a mastermind group solely for self-employed people. I was feeling itchy to move my business to the next level, knowing that there was something bigger out there for me, but not having the right kind of group support to break through the creativity blocks and emotional uncertainty.

So, in January 2003, I sent an invitation to everyone on my mailing list to join a Self-Employed Success Mastermind Group. I asked people to fill out a 10-question application and included what I thought was the most important question of all: "Why should you be chosen to participate in this group?" I was looking for people who were deeply committed to the idea of growing their businesses, and themselves as human beings, and were willing to both give help and ask for help in a group setting.

I received 53 applications, and in February 2003 chose 20 people to participate, divided into two groups. Because these applicants were from all over the globe, the groups were set up to "meet" via an online message board.

I had five years' experience facilitating message groups on two of CompuServe's largest forums in the mid-'90s, which helped me prepare for facilitating mastermind groups virtually. I precreated many conversation-starter questions and uploaded one a week to the message board to keep things active. In addition, each week members were to share their success stories (no matter how big or small the successes) and create and reply to requests for brainstorming on challenges, problems, and decisions. A requirement of the group was that each member must participate at least once a week.

Gradually, as happens with many mastermind groups, some people dropped out and some we had to "fire" from the group for lack of participation or always asking for help but never offering it to others. The purpose, and success, of a mastermind group relies on people being firmly committed to participating actively in the group and in the give and take of brainstorming.

When people started in the group, they honestly felt they were ready to grow their business and face their self-sabotaging behavior. However, members soon discovered that the group wouldn't tolerate bad behavior and repeatedly missing goals. The group was simply too demanding for some, while others flourished in the atmosphere.

The group reinvented itself later that year by combining the two groups into one and limiting it to women only. In early 2004, we evolved again by opting to have a 90-minute monthly teleconference call as the backbone of communication. Now we meet on the third Thursday of each month in a conference call and continue to have daily conversations on the message board. It's not uncommon for us to be logged in at the same time, answering messages as soon as someone else posts one!

Over time, other self-employed women have found our group through word of mouth, some found us through Google, and others were colleagues of existing members. When new women want to join, they fill out an application. The group reviews the applications, rejecting some and asking some applicants to come on our monthly call to introduce themselves. We then vote on who can join. Group consensus is crucial to our success; all the members have a say in what happens to the group.

Today, we keep our group size to five or six members, which is about all that can be accommodated on a 90-minute phone call. The current participants include Pamela Zurek, a graphic designer; Dr. Susan Burger, a chiropractor; Katherine Scott, a vocal coach; Jamie Novak, a professional organizer, author, and creator of products for QVC; and myself, Karyn Greenstreet, a small business coach and self-employment expert. We're from across the United States and Canada and have all been in business at least 10 years, so we're well past the bumpy "new business phase" and ready to move to the next level.

We've never met in person as a group, and most members have never met each other in person.

Though we come from different countries and professions, it's utterly amazing how we always seem to be having the same personal and business growth challenges, just in different guises. This year, for instance, we're all working on allowing the universe to bring us opportunities instead of feeling that we need to control and orchestrate every minute aspect of our future success. We're all opening up to new ways of perceiving our businesses and how our businesses reflect our personal values, which helps us all answer the question "What's next?" for our businesses.

Over the years, we've been involved in each other's lives and businesses to a very deep extent. We've seen each other through business highs and lows, decisions to move across country, divorces, deaths, and celebrations. We've supported and encouraged each other through painful business decisions and the joy and satisfaction of big contracts and the completion of big projects.

For me, the overall benefits are brainstorming with the group and the group helping me maintain integrity with my goals and values. Masterminding with others gives me emotional support when I'm feeling freaked out by work or when I'm feeling excited about a new project idea. The group holds my feet to the fire, which I need. I also enjoy our spirituality talks and how spirituality relates to our personal and business lives in real, concrete ways.

We use a bridge line service for our monthly teleconferences and a Yahoo Groups message board (http://groups.yahoo.com) for daily communication. We like Yahoo Groups because it allows both e-mail delivery and web-based delivery, and each member can set her own delivery preferences. Yahoo Groups also allows us to upload photos of ourselves, as well as files that we want the group to review and critique.

Being virtual and communicating via message board and teleconference is perfect for us. For instance, I get a lot of e-mail and don't want any additional e-mail crowding my in-box, so I prefer to read and respond to messages online. Jamie and I are night owls, and it's not uncommon to see messages from us at 11:00 at night. Susan has a busy practice and two children; she gets her messages both at the office and at home, so she can read and respond whenever she has a few minutes. Jamie travels on book tours, but because we're a virtual group, she's able to participate from whichever town she lands in. Katherine is about to move from Toronto to Vancouver (on the other side of Canada), but she'll still have the group to support her as she moves her home and business 3,000 miles away.

There are some real benefits to meeting via teleconference and message board. As Pamela puts it, "I think our group is special because it is virtual. Because we communicate by e-mail and phone calls, there is an element of anonymity. I know a lot has been written about how people abuse the anonymity that the Internet offers, but in this case I think it allows us to reveal more about what's going on in our businesses and lives in an environment that feels safe. That level of communication leads to a feeling of support and friendship that is quite genuine, despite the distances between us."

This year, we're having a Mastermind Retreat Weekend at my house in the countryside, which will be the first time we've all met each other in person as a group. We're all excited and nervous to finally meet face-to-face! Over the course of four days, we'll meet in live mastermind sessions, and each member has agreed to teach a two-hour class on a topic of her expertise that the group will find valuable. Because this is the first time we've met in person, we've scheduled lots of time for relaxing in the hot tub, wandering my 3.5 acres, journaling, meditating, and enjoying meals together.

You can find out more about Karyn Greenstreet by visiting www.passionforbusiness.com.

8

THE IMAGINARY MASTERMIND GROUP

A little group of wise hearts is better than a wilderness of fools.

—John Ruskin

In his 1928 book, *The Law of Success,* Napoleon Hill tells the story of a close friend who was a well-known writer and public speaker. Before achieving his success, the man created a new twist on the mastermind concept.

Every night, he would close his eyes and visualize a table in a conference room. Seated around the table were Abraham Lincoln, George Washington, Napoleon Bonaparte, Ralph Waldo Emerson, and Elbert Hubbard.[1]

---

[1] Elbert Hubbard was a famous magazine publisher in the late 1890s through the early 1900s. He's said to have published more than 7 million words. Prior to being a writer, Hubbard was the head of sales and advertising for one of the most successful mail order houses in the country. Hubbard introduced the idea of adding premium merchandise to induce people to buy his clients' products. He also started a plan that made each customer a potential

The man would speak to each of these members of his imaginary mastermind in turn. The conversation went something like this:

Mr. Lincoln, I wish to build into my own character the patience, fairness, and sense of humor that were the cornerstones of your personality.

Mr. Bonaparte, I wish to build into my own character the self-reliance and ability to conquer obstacles and to turn defeat into victory as you've done.

Mr. Washington, I wish to develop the spirit of patriotism, self-sacrifice, and leadership that you were well-known for.

Mr. Emerson, I wish to develop the vision, appreciation, and understanding of the laws of nature that were your outstanding characteristics.

Mr. Hubbard, I wish to possess your ability to express yourself in clear, concise, and forceful language.

Gentlemen, I will not be satisfied until I've developed these qualities for myself.

For several months, this man met with his imaginary mastermind group. Eventually, he found that he'd established each of their desired characteristics

---

salesman. He may well be the originator of affiliate marketing. He may well be the originator of affiliate marketing. Hubbard and his wife died at sea with the sinking of the Lusitania in 1915.

in his own personality. He credited his imaginary mastermind as one of the keys of his success.

Why not try this yourself?

Sure, it may seem a bit weird. I can hear you now: "Bill, only little kids have imaginary friends." So what if it sounds silly? Nobody has to know but you.

And think about it. You can have anyone you want in your imaginary mastermind.

If you want to grow your business, you could choose from the greatest business minds of all time. You could "invite" Andrew Carnegie, Henry Ford, Walt Disney, Ray Kroc, J.P. Morgan, John D. Rockefeller, Sam Walton, Bill Gates, or Michael Dell.

If you want to improve your golf game, you could form a mastermind group with Tiger Woods, Jack Nicklaus, Arnold Palmer, Walter Hagen, and Bobby Jones.

If you want to write a great novel, why not ask J.K. Rowling, Jane Austen, Stephen King, Leo Tolstoy, and Mark Twain to join your group?

Joe is a hypnotherapist who says this "invisible mastermind" is actually brilliant. He holds these mental conversations with famous bodybuilders from the past, such as Steve Reeves (who played Hercules in the movies). Joe says your unconscious mind is a vast storehouse of ideas and resources. When you create a mental mastermind, you open the door to this rich inner frontier.

I've had a taste of success with this as well, although by a slightly different method. Carl Galletti, an expert copywriter, taught me that I could develop a style similar to that of any writer I chose simply by copying his or her work in longhand. Joe does the same thing.

I've tried this with some successful sales letters and it works. I've also found that if I listen frequently to books and seminars on audiotapes, I tend to absorb the expertise of the speaker.

That's also how I developed the knack for doing web site reviews that led to MasterSiteReviewer.com . (Web site owners come to my site for critiques to help increase their sales.) I listened to other copywriters doing critiques so often that I absorbed their styles to the point I became an expert myself.

Although an imaginary mastermind group is not a substitute for the real thing, it can be a powerful tool for adding the qualities and characteristics of the supersuccessful in any field you wish to pursue.

Why not make a list right here of the famous people you would invite into your mastermind?

[space left intentionally blank in the original book]

9

OTHER VIEWS OF MASTERMINDS

We must all hang together, or assuredly, we shall all hang separately.

—Benjamin Franklin

In this chapter, we'd like to share other people's experiences with masterminds. These stories can provide ideas for ways you might run your own group, point out potential pitfalls, and serve as inspiration.

A GROUP OF TWO

Barbara Johnson

My friend Diane and I formed a Mastermind Writing Group, via e-mail and regular mail, two years ago. We have both finished the first drafts of our novels. This year our goals are to get two edits done of the books, and then do the proposals and mail them out to at least five publishers or agents.

I have wanted to be a mystery novel writer for at least 30 years. I talked about it, I read magazines about it, and I went to writing conferences. With the dawn of the Internet I joined writing classes online.

I wrote short pieces for the newspaper and for church bulletins and, of course, letters to the editor. Novel writing was still a dream. Then, two years ago, I was whining to my friend in Arizona about never getting the time to write my great novel. She had the same problem. She read the books and the magazines, too. She had the dream. We made our own mastermind group. We are accountability partners. We have to write at least one print letter a week and e-mail as often as necessary. Once a month we send each other goals with dates and then hold ourselves accountable. This has helped us both keep the writing goals fresh and in our minds. With our e-mails we share things we learn, articles we find, good words, ideas, anything and everything. More than anything, this group of two has kept me writing and on track with writing goals.

A MASTERMIND MIRACLE

Marianne St. Clair (www.mariannestclair.com)

In forming a mastermind group I was able to do many things that would not have been possible otherwise. I was diagnosed with a tumor a few years ago and several doctors wanted to do a hysterectomy to remove the tumor. I was 33 and the mother of beautiful daughter, but I was not ready to give up my ability to have more children in the future. I decided to mastermind for a different outcome. I created $17,000 in 30 hours from people donating out of the blue to me. I flew to Boston and had a surgeon perform a myomectomy. I now have a second beautiful daughter as a result of my success with masterminding.

PERSISTENCE PAYS OFF

Kenneth Koh (www.subconscious-secrets.com)

I started forming my mastermind group in 2001, after attending a course in masterminding. Since then, I've quit my job and started two businesses. The beginning was difficult. When I formed my first mastermind group, it didn't last three months. After the course, everyone was highly motivated. We met up once a week, brainstorming on various business ideas. Eventually, we decided on one idea and we acted on it! That was when things started to go wrong.

As we began work on the business idea, one member started to doubt its feasibility. That's when the harmony within the group started to disintegrate. Another member complained that he was doing most of the work. Soon, reality set in. Everyone was busy with their full-time job (or was it just an excuse?). We were so busy that it became harder and harder to find a time to meet. Finally, we had one last meeting, when we managed to convince ourselves that the business idea was not feasible. That was the end of my first mastermind experience.

Since then, I learned that I have to choose my mastermind team carefully. I have to find people who are already in the industry that my business is in so that I can leverage their existing network and strength while I add in my brains.

My first successful mastermind group started in 2003—that's two years later! Persistence pays. It really pays. This time, I wanted to start a distribution business. My mastermind team is a group of individuals with more than 10 years of experience in distribution. Finding the right team makes things so much easier.

The business took off and in a short while started working by itself, mainly because I leveraged the existing business network of my partners. That gave me more time to explore other business opportunities. Since then, I rarely do things on my own because masterminding makes things so much easier, better, and faster.

I have realized recently that masterminding can also be performed without meeting each other face-to-face, thanks to the Internet! When I started my web site, www.subconscious-secrets.com, I seriously ran out of ideas to write. So I started asking my newsletter subscribers to ask me questions and interact with me. The result was amazing. I could accomplish so much more in much less time.

Masterminding has allowed me to do MORE with LESS. Some of the lessons I've learned from masterminding:

1. Harmony is the key. There must be a common agenda, a common goal.

2. All the members must be selfless. Don't work with a group of people who are financially poor, or people without a financial abundance mentality. Those types of people are always thinking "How can I make more from you?" instead of "How can we make more as a whole?"

3. Be the one to go the extra mile and contribute more. Someone has got to walk the talk first before others will follow.

A BEST-SELLING AUTHOR AND A DREAM FOR CHILDREN AND THEIR PARENTS REALIZED

Megan Orlando
(www.familymediationsolutions.com)

My mastermind group provided me a safety net of support. Their regular support enabled me to take risks; to envision my goals in high definition instead of black and white; to dream bigger dreams so as to keep pace with my willingness to grow. My mastermind partners helped me stay focused while still enjoying the investigation and realization of my dreams. As a result of my mastermind group I have become a best-selling author and coauthor with Dr. Wayne Dyer and Dr. Deepak Chopra and other professionals *(Giving Gratitude)*.

My story addresses the use of mediation to resolve child abuse, neglect, abandonment, and divorce trauma for children and parents. The children and parents with whom I have the privilege of working have shown me by their willingness to open up and share their stories how courage to grow can overcome adversity. When we open our hearts and minds, hear each other's stories, we can discover more possibility for growth within ourselves. Where there is gratitude we are able to encourage one another to be brave and grow, to experience more compassion, learn to communicate better, and overcome our conflicts with one another. When we experience gratitude we have the power to make new choices and behave better toward each other.

The mastermind process encouraged each of us to share our own stories and to build new dreams. Once dreamed, these bigger choices became possible for each of us. For me, it enabled me to envision helping children and parents everywhere by making the promise of mediation known beyond the walls of the courthouse so more families can make better choices.

THE ONLY OPTION MASTERMIND GROUP

Paul Simoneau (www.theonlyoption.net)

Imagine standing in the middle of the energy of a class-5 tornado. This is the huge energy that is truly a "finger of God." Feel that power and know all the way down to your toes that individually and as a group, you can focus it to be whatever you desire. With that clearly in your heart and mind, you have the mastermind feeling. I am truly blessed to share the growing synergy and power of the mastermind group The Only Option.

Al, Annie, Christina, David, Mary, and I are all part of a larger group of like-hearted people working with Joe Vitale's book *The Attractor Factor.* Al Diaz invited us, and some others, to join him in fulfilling Joe's suggested mission to "Dare Something Worthy" and make the world a better place.

Over time the group became six of the most creative, motivated, caring people I have ever had the pleasure to know. We quickly developed, and keep, our mastermind mission right out in front to guide our steps. We enhance love and life by sharing our gifts in guiding others to the best and highest good of all, the only option.

In just three holiday-filled months, we have collaborated to complete an ebook, *The Titus Concept: Money, for My Best and Highest Good;* a web site to make it available to the world; an audio version of that same book (I am honored to have read it), produced by The Only Option Mastermind Group and provided as a companion to the ebook; a rapidly expanding community that shares; a soon-to-be-published hard copy version of the ebook; a daily inspirational e-mail to lead the community "Forward to a Better Day"; a soon-to-be-announced mentoring program that offers protégés the full power of The Only Option Mastermind Group to guide them; and much more that will pour out benefits for our Best and Highest Good for years to come.

Mark Victor Hansen is right: "One plus one, doesn't equal two. It becomes the power of eleven." Something amazing and magical happens when a group of people combine their skills, talents, abilities, and dreams to reach a common constellation and go way past swinging on a single star.

Our six-pack takes that to another realm by creating exponentially greater synergy and synchronicity. It has become an upwardly spiraling, ever expanding field of unlimited potential. The intangible accomplishments are already blooming. Each of us has new offerings incubating in The Only Option.

We continue to grow as this mastermind group energizes each member to reach new heights and to stride boldly beyond where our individual dreams would be years from now. The power of the mastermind also spreads outside the six members to family, friends, coworkers, and even strangers who notice an invigorating life force expanding into their personal space.

Take firm charge of the life you desire and require. Know that we are all part of the ultimate Mastermind of life, for our Best and Highest Good. It is The Only Option.

A 19-YEAR-OLD USES MASTERMINDS TO BE-COME A TEEN FORCE TO BE RECKONED WITH

Muhammad Shariq (www.SecretsoftheMillionDollarMan.com)

A mastermind group is what takes you to the next level.

For me, a mastermind group changed my life 180 degrees. It helped me learn immensely, have support of successful people, have the courage to make things happen, think big, and helped me become a "bigger" person.

When I joined a network marketing organization at the age of 16, our group was the fastest growing new group. The reason: We masterminded twice a week. We helped each other become bigger. We brainstormed how we can reach a bigger audience. We kicked each other to make sure we were all on the right track.

The mastermind brainstorm sessions were the most profitable because we were people on the same mental wavelength; all 10 people bent on finding the answer increases the success chances by 10! And it was because of that mastermind group that I was able to earn my first network marketing check (my first income) at 16!

Later I became part of a bigger mastermind group. All the people in that group were more successful than I. People who had founded big business and network marketing companies, people who had 30 to 40 years of marketing experience, people who had traveled all over the world. There I just became a sponge.

I learned from each and every one of them as much as I could. The things I learned in an hour from across the table could take a year of study if I had to learn them myself! I also assisted them as best I could.

I helped them organize events, sell their training packages (on commission, of course), and just helped them however I could. In return they didn't decline when I needed some help.

At times I felt I was the one who was benefiting the MOST from this group! I was too young and too small to be in that group, but they let me in because I acted BIG. I had BIG dreams, courage, and the guts to do BIG stuff and just the desire to be BIG and to be among BIG people. So they let me in.

Many times I spent the mastermind meetings absolutely quiet, just listening to them because they were talking about something out of my caliber. So I learned from just listening to their conversations. This just shows that being in a mastermind group that's light years ahead of you is not impossible. If you have a burning desire and are action-orientated, people, no matter how BIG they are, appreciate you and you get a chance to get closer and learn from them.

Before becoming a part of that group, I was almost unknown. Being in that group helped me become known. And the contacts I developed and the people I met because of being a part of that group were awesome! I can't even list the dozens and dozens of mind-blowing, successful people I met. Like the founder of the fastest growing network marketing company of 2003, the author of the first book on network marketing in Pakistan, a multimillionaire investor, people who had started from below zero, who were NOTHING 30 to 40 years ago, but have reached unimaginable heights today.

So my contacts grew. People came to know me better. They invited me to other events, meetings, and seminars. This is just an added bonus to being in a mastermind. Moreover, the relationships I made, the bonds that I made with the people there, they are life-lasting. I can be sure that I have a support system behind me. People I can trust to lean on, people who can advise me when I need it most, who can help me pick myself up when I've fallen down, people who are there to buck me up and believe in me.

And it's not just in network marketing. Even after I left network marketing, what I had learned from the mastermind meetings helped me grow as a person. Now I have my own mastermind group, known as Teen Force Group. Basically, I founded an organization known as TEEN FORCE, whose main focus is to have mastermind groups around the world for teens and young people who come together to help each other make it BIG in life.

It's already running, but I plan to launch it publicly by 2008. Also, by the end of this year, I'll have an online mastermind group for young and successful ONLINE business entrepreneurs. We'll help young people like ourselves and others make it BIG ONLINE with chat sessions every week or alternate week.

Right now, I'm part of two main mastermind groups. One is where all the other people in the group are more successful than I. I am the youngest, least experienced, and less successful than the others. I basically learn (a ton!) from being there. The other is my local Teen Force Group.

We teens discuss and help each other to make it BIG in life. I'm the most successful person in this group. So I let others learn from me and of course we help each other get the best out of ourselves and be a BIG success in life.

Side note: It's important to be a part of both kinds of mastermind groups. Being in a group of people who are as successful as you or just a little more or less helps you be close with the rest. You can all talk as if you're on the same level and push each other for the better when needed. That can't happen in a group where everyone else is more successful than you. There the air is different and beneficial in other ways. Both are necessary, in my opinion.

I can't tell enough about the benefits of being in a mastermind group. I feel like I can write a whole book on it! I also got the courage of doing things I never thought were possible for me before. I convinced an investor, who I had close contact with, to invest on a big business plan I have for 2007.

I never thought any investor would take a 19-year-old seriously and invest his money in the idea. But it happened to me! Thanks to the contact from the mastermind group and the confidence I got from them.

I also helped my partners in their special events and seminars and learned a lot about this business. So, a year ago in December 2004, I organized and hosted my own International Seminar! And I'm just 19!

These are just a few of things that I achieved, a lot more than I can count but that made me the person I am today. If I can achieve this much being in a mastermind group at 19 I can just imagine where I'll be after 10 years of being in such mastermind groups! Imagine! And get ready to become a part of or start your own mastermind group!

TAP, TAP, TAP ... IT'S YOUR MASTERMIND CALLING

Brad Yates (www.moneybeyondbelief.com)

By all accounts, this has been the best year for me ever career wise. And while there are many factors that have contributed to this success, there is one glaring thing that I started doing just before the biggest changes started occurring in my life.

I joined a mastermind group.

Napoleon Hill talks about making use of OPM and OPB, or Other People's Money and Other People's Brains. Although the first is both important and generally necessary in new and/or large ventures, I believe the second to be even more valuable. There is a reason for the saying "Two heads are better than one." And more is better—up to a point. Experts suggest a group should consist of 8 to 12 members.

I've been involved with different types of mastermind groups before, but never with as much structure as the one with which I am currently involved. It was originally set up as part of a coaching program with Bob Proctor, author of *You Were Born Rich* and a top sales and prosperity trainer. Bob has put a number of these groups together and has a questionnaire by which he determines who should be with whom in the mastermind partnerships.

Bob also has mastermind principles and a template for a successful process. This keeps the weekly calls moving in a productive manner so that folks get the most out of the process. The calls begin with a reading of the principles so that the participants are grounded and on the same page. Then members take turns relating their wins for the week, as well as their challenges and needs from the group. Other members then offer support as appropriate, such as a statement of positive intention for the person or a referral to a potential business contact.

This process had helped to keep me focused on what I am up to. There is a level of accountability—but in a different way from when I am working with a coach. There is an opportunity to get feedback from a number of people who, though perhaps not trained coaches, have expertise in different areas. My current group has folks from a variety of different professions, income levels (from still struggling to multimillionaire), and even countries. But all are committed to success and growth.

Obviously, the success of any group is dependent on the members. The first mastermind group I was with fizzled out in a matter of a month or two, until only 2 of the original 12 were attending the calls. The other remaining member and I, determined to get the most from the process, got ourselves into another group. Although not everyone can make the call every week, the consistency of at least a core group has been impressive. No one is paid to be there—we call in to support our team and to be likewise supported.

And it works.

After a few months with this group, I found the courage to leave the security of a day job and pursue my real passion. Within six more months, I had more than tripled my income. The other members have also related increases in both financial and personal success.

I have also had the opportunity to be of service in my own unique way, introducing EFT [Emotional Freedom Technique] to a group of professionals who might not have otherwise found this process. On a few occasions throughout the year I have conducted tapping sessions for the group to clear abundance issues.[2]

It is difficult to pinpoint exactly what amount of my success is due to being involved in the mastermind process, but it is no doubt a crucial element. For those who know the Law of Attraction, you know that thinking and feeling positively brings good things into your life. The mastermind process provides a weekly opportunity to get support in being in that successful state of mind.

If you are not doing this yet—a process that is recommended by most, if not all, of the great success teachers—then please tap with me: "Even though I am resisting masterminding...."

MASTERMIND GROUPS PROVIDE CONFIDENCE AND FOCUS

Mindy Hurt-Audin (www.unityofwimberley.com)

---

[2] EFT is a technique involving tapping with the fingertips, various parts of the body to relieve stress, anxiety, fears and trauma. In this instance, Brad is referring to mental blocks that group members have over possessing an abundance of money.

I've been in lots of mastermind groups. Some of them with professionals in my industry that met weekly, some of them very goal-oriented that met weekly, and my longest running group is simply a very good friend in San Francisco who calls each week for a personal and professional check-in.

I can't think of any earth-shattering results that I've had as a part of a group. But I will say this: Being involved in mastermind groups gave me the confidence and the focus I needed to launch my own business, to quit my old job, and to be able to live my dream as a professional speaker. It's a lot easier to step onto the game field when you've got coaches and cheerleaders supporting you from the sidelines.

THE MOST POWERFUL MASTERMIND: "THE PSYCHIC MASTERMIND"

Dave Boufford, Mr. Positive

I first learned of the mastermind principle from Napoleon Hill in the classic book *Think and Grow Rich.*

The mastermind I'm going to share is a little different from the ones you may have read about in the previous pages. It really falls into what Napoleon Hill described as the "psychic phase of the Mastermind," and it's my hope that this will provide you with an additional way to apply this powerful concept in your life.

Over the years I have been involved in several mastermind groups. Most had two to five members. They were designed strictly for achieving specific business goals. But the most powerful alliance I ever formed is my current mastermind with my partner in life, my wife, Arlene.

There are a few reasons I think this is the most powerful form of a mastermind:

1. *Common goals:* We are both in precise alignment with our long-term vision and mission. We know where we want to go and how we would like to travel.
2. *Different strengths:* We both bring different strengths to our mastermind. She's very analytical and practical and I'm a dreamer, a big thinker, who sees all the possibilities.
3. *Chemistry:* There's harmony and synergy in being together.
4. *Love:* Our mastermind is an outgrowth of the love, respect, and admiration we have for one another.

The way it works: We started out quite informally with a planning session each January where we would outline our personal goals and, both being entrepreneurs, we would outline our business goals, too.

At least once a month we would get together and discuss our progress toward our objectives and review any adjustments that we needed to make.

We worked great together this way for a couple of years, and then a change in direction for me really opened up the power of the mastermind we had formed.

I'll skip all the details, but after consulting with my mastermind partner, it was decided that I would leave the business I had spent the previous three and a half years building and venture out after my dream of creating a new alternative news service, PNN-Positive News Network (www.positivenews.net).

I have started several businesses over the years, but I had never pursued this dream full time as a business and it was quite a leap of faith for Arlene to support me in this pursuit.

However, up until the time I stepped out into the unknown I did not realize how much power our mastermind alliance held. If you have ever started a business in a totally new field from your previous work you may understand how scary and challenging it can be.

The strength, wisdom, patience, and encouragement I received from my mastermind partner continues to pull me through.

There have been difficult times during the past 18 months when walking away and getting a regular paycheck would have made sense both economically and emotionally, but my mastermind partner kept me going.

Having my mastermind partner to provide input, advice, and emotional support has been an incredibly humbling experience. Our mastermind has kept me focused and motivated to climb this mountain.

In addition to my dream business being realized, this mastermind experience has had another incredible benefit: It has deepened and strengthened our relationship and love for one another beyond what I have words for.

Now don't rush out to get married to build a mastermind like ours. Just be open to the possibility of forming a "Psychic Mastermind" with someone who truly loves and believes in you.*

[* Dave Boufford is known as "Mr. Positive" and is the founder of PNN-Positive News Network. PNN currently publishes a daily e-zine called Positive News, which is read by more than 10,000 people in 120 countries. You can find "Mr. Positive" on the Internet at www.PositiveNews.net.]

THE EBOOK COACH

Ellen Violette (SellMoreEbooks.com)

When I first got online, I had a mailing list of about 40 people. I hired a coach, Matt Bacak, to help me build my list and he had a mastermind group for his clients. One of his list-building strategies was to do bonus giveaways. We've done three so far. The first one built my list by 200 e-mails, the next one netted 230 new e-mails, and the last one brought in 441. And the bonus offers just keep growing.

I've also found three joint venture partners so far, and one of those, Matt Zembruski, has become my mastermind buddy. We have a regular call once a week and we share information, strategies, opportunities, and resources—we also cheer each other on!

My relationship with Matt has been invaluable in my business. In fact, he is now one of my closest friends. Another one of my joint venture partners from the mastermind group, Todd Reese, is "The Internet Auction Specialist." He is now helping me get my digital products on eBay and I am helping him become more visible on the Internet. I've introduced both Matt and Todd to Jim Edwards, and now they have both contributed bonuses to an ebook that I am writing with Jim called *Sell More eBooks! Low & No Cost Tactics to Explode Your eBook Sales & Downloads.*

I also find the mastermind group very helpful as a way for people with different backgrounds and talents to share information and cross-pollinate. My husband, Christen Violette, founder of Creative Mind Training, has gotten bonuses for his products from other group members. We help people promote their offers and they help us. We've also learned about software, products, upcoming conferences, and other opportunities that can help our businesses that we wouldn't have known about otherwise.

We recently participated in helping Matt Bacak take his new book, *The Ultimate Lead Generation*

Plan, to number one on Barnes and Noble and Amazon and raised over $20,000 for Habitat for Humanity, which felt pretty amazing!

I have found this mastermind group to be so valuable that I have started one for my eBook Profit Marketing Program. Once someone goes through my program he or she can join the mastermind group as well, and my clients really appreciate having that opportunity to connect with me on an ongoing basis as well as with each other to continue to work together and grow their businesses.

I believe mastermind groups are a fabulous place to forge business relationships as well as personal friendships, share information, cross promote, and foster creative ideas and solutions for your business. I highly recommend them to anyone who is serious about leveraging his or her time and energy into a highly successful business.

I DON'T NEED TO KNOW YOU. I KNOW MARK.

Mark Weisser

I don't need to know you. I know Mark.

—Frank Hathorn, vice president Lockwood Bank

These words still make the hairs on my arms stand up. Dan Valdez, at the time owner of Stationery &

Furnishings in Houston, quoted my banker's words to me one day after Dan had a phone conversation with him. My banker was Frank Hathorn.

Frank was one of those rare bankers, what I would call a relationship banker. For Frank, your word was your bond and the paperwork was for the file (and the bank examiners).

What I am about to tell you is a perfect illustration of the hidden power of a mastermind group and what it can do.

If you have a minute, let me tell you what happened.

Even better, let Dan tell you in his words—straight from him to you.

It was a fine Monday about 5:15P.M. and I was on my way home when I got the call on my cell phone. I looked down and saw my banker's number on the little screen.

I thought it sort of odd that she would call me so late in the day, so I just had to answer. After the chitchat, she informed me in no uncertain terms that the bank was not going to renew my note and they were calling it in. In three days. Just like that.

If you aren't familiar with that term, that means they require you to pay it off. In total. In cash. By whatever means. And they can do that. (Read your loan documents.)

After the initial shock began to wear off, my first question was, "What did I do to cause this? You cannot be serious."

She assured me that, no, I didn't cause this and, yes, she was serious.

I hung up the phone and thought about it. There was absolutely no way I could come up with enough to pay the note. A hundred and fifty grand? No way.

All my cash was tied up in inventory and prepayments for inventory. Most of that night I paced the floor, facing an almost overwhelming fear.

As the night progressed, I felt like I was faced with losing everything: my livelihood, my family's security, and our very existence. It was a fear that I had never experienced before—or since, for that matter. No sleep, no relief, tremendous fear and anxiety.

Morning came, as it always does. I was exhausted and I wanted to stay home. Just give up and take the next steps to the inevitable bankruptcy. Life as I knew it was about to change abruptly.

I was supposed to get up early and attend my mastermind group. We called it a roundtable, but it is the same thing. I have to tell you that was the last thing I wanted to do. I just wanted to bury my head in the covers and pretend it would all just go away.

But years of business ownership instill a sense of responsibility, and these were people I had known a long time and they counted on me to be there. So off I went, thinking that surely this would be a waste of time because no one at that meeting could understand my predicament, much less offer any immediate relief for my helpless situation.

But then, I thought maybe at least I could get some relief by telling the story to the group and get some sympathy and personal emotional support. I got to the meeting and told everyone what happened and I got just what I thought, a strong sense of support but no real relief for the money problem. I left and went to my office to face the next step in my company's demise.

Then, right at 10:00, my phone rang and the voice said, "Hi, Dan, my name is Frank Hathorn and I am with Lockwood Bank and I understand you have a problem with your bank."

He then said that he heard all about this from my friend and fellow roundtable member, Mark Weisser.

We talked a bit and he then said, "You go call your bank and tell them that we will pay off that note. I will take care of the paperwork within the next few days."

I thought I was dreaming, or perhaps I passed into another world! And then I said, "Frank, I know how banks work—how can you do this? You don't know me or anything about my company or my credit worthiness."

His resounding words were simple and profound: "I don't need to know you, I know Mark."

The next day the money was wired to my bank, paying off my loan.

Those words are as real today as they were all those years ago. Quickly, I learned the power of a group of people who dedicate themselves to helping each other in good times and bad. People who listen, challenge, offer help, and take action when it counts the most.

Today, Mark is still my friend and ultimate supporter. He and the other members of that roundtable were all there when I buried my wife and there for all the good times as well. We have all been there when it counted most. We still care about each other's success and personal futures. I thank God every day for these people and that roundtable group.

See what I mean?

I am the Mark Weisser in that story and the way Dan tells it still gets to me.

So that's an illustration of the power of a mastermind group, sometimes called roundtables, and there are other titles as well.

Mastermind groups are small—four to eight participants would be ideal. The goal of such a group is to support each other in business and personally. Respect and trust are the bonds that keep the group functioning. They will be board members of your company when they need to be, asking the tough questions, and sympathetic shoulders to lean on when they need to be, when a spouse dies.

They are the ones you trust to work through tough times. Employee embezzlement, a pregnant team leader during a crisis, drugs in the shop. They are the ones to ask for help in structuring a sale of your company or to seek advice for your next book.

That all sounds good, right? So how do you form one?

Here are a few guidelines to consider:

- People have to be matched by personalities and how they blend. You put people together who seem to fit together, and then you let the group dynamics work out who stays and who goes.
- Once established, the group has to vote unanimously on every additional member.
- What is said in a roundtable stays there. This is a cardinal rule.
- At every meeting, everyone does a check-in to communicate news since the previous meeting.
- In turn (unless there is a special situation) members take their place on the "Hot Seat" and present their own situation, requesting help and advice from the group.
- The group holds the member accountable for accomplishing the tasks that evolve from that meeting.
- Communication and contact between meetings is critical to the group's success.
- One-on-one get-togethers between members and between roundtable meetings is essential to the growth of the personal relationships that make the group synergistic.
- One member of the group should be selected to chair and lead the group so that the necessary continuity and adherence to the process is maintained.

- A day and time for every month/week should be selected by the group for meeting, and the time should be treated by every member as sacred. To miss a meeting once in a while is okay, but repeated misses are grounds for dismissal of a member from the group.
- There is a standard meeting agenda that is followed. The time during a meeting should be used effectively and the group must work to avoid purely social interaction so that the essential business can be transacted and the serious issues get covered when they arise.

Let me close here with one more quick story. It's mine and it's not very long.

I have been in a business club called the Dover Club for 15 years now. It's in Houston, Texas, which is a great place for entrepreneurs of all types. The club functions like a large mastermind group but encourages subgroups to form that are called roundtables, or mastermind groups.

Many years ago, I had a lunch meeting with another member, Donna Fisher. She had just written a book, and as I was interested in getting into writing on a professional basis, I just had to visit with her about the process.

She spent most of the lunch talking about this fantastic writer who coached her through the process of not only writing the book, but what to do with it when she finished it. "You need to meet him," she told me. "Let me call him for you and I will introduce you to him."

She did.

I met this writer, got to know this writer, learned from this writer, and befriended this writer.

This writer is Joe Vitale.

Multiply your talent and ability. Form or join a mastermind group.

It works.

SOMETIMES YOU HAVE TO PAY TO PLAY

Amy Looper and Beth Carls, Cofounders, Mind OH! and Or Better Performance Group

Recently, a new twist on mastermind groups has evolved and it's called an "Inner Circle." The Inner Circle term has been referenced before. It is a group of people who care about you and will be there for you. It can be personal or business focused.

You may remember a recent reference to Inner Circles in the very funny movie Ben Stiller starred in a few years ago called *Meet the Fockers.* Ben Stiller plays a character whose father-in-law, played by Robert De Niro, is suspicious of him and tests Ben to see if he has what it takes to not only marry his daughter but to then be accepted into the family's "Inner Circle."

Another Inner Circle application my business partner, Beth Carls, and I have recently participated in for 18 months as charter members is called the Enlightened Millionaire Institute's Inner Circle. There, 100 entrepreneurs from around the world have been personally mentored by Mark Victor Hansen and Robert G. Allen. You recognize these names because Mark Victor Hansen is the phenomenal cocreator of the *Chicken Soup for the Soul* series and Robert G. Allen is one of the world's foremost financial and real estate experts.

This newer iteration of a larger Inner Circle includes a fee, and you're mentored, usually by well-known subject matter experts. Typically, there are weekly group teleconference calls because these super Inner Circles can attract people from literally everywhere. A private password-protected web-based discussion forum and other technology-based tools are used to keep the group connected. In our Inner Circle experience, we participated in quarterly three-to seven-day group meetings at designated venues around the world to round out our experience.

We called these meetings "immersives" because we were literally immersed in learning from Bob and Mark and through breakout sessions with other Inner Circle members as well as well-known guests. As you can tell already, an experience like this is a huge commitment in time and money. But that's what the "pay to play" Inner Circles mean—the highest of expectations and results to move forward quickly, whether it is for creating a new idea or speed-to-market of an existing product or service.

Our decision to participate in a "pay to play" Inner Circle made sense to my partner and me to have access to these two very successful entrepreneurs and their Inner Circle of business associates. In other words, we wanted to up-level and rapidly expand our network with other successful people (and their networks) in ways we could not have otherwise done one-to-one!

In Mark and Bob's first book, *The One Minute Millionaire,* they identified that most millionaires share a certain set of characteristics and similar processes that's translated into huge success.

They call their three-stage process the "Millionaire Equation": **Dream+A Team+A Theme=Millionaire Streams.** Imagine this for a minute. Maybe you want to have more business success, maybe more personal success, maybe you want to leave a nonchallenging job and start your own business, or maybe you like your current job and you just want to move up the corporate ladder. Imagine anything you want right this very instant and simply hold this thought in your mind for a minute.... Have you got it?

Write it in the space below. (Beth and I did this exercise and in a few minutes I'm going to share with you what all has happened for our business just with this simple exercise and our Inner Circle team.) Go ahead, imagine for a minute...

[space left intentionally blank in the original book]

Okay, now ask yourself "How 'fast' can I get _____ right this very minute?"

Well, now that you have your dream written down, next is having your own personal team or Inner Circle of powerful individuals with the desire, commitment, and contacts to help you *leverage* your dream to make it happen. And in many cases, as was our experience, make it happen sooner *or better* than you could on your own!

Here's Mark and Bob's definition of an Inner Circle from their newest book, *Cracking the Millionaire Code:* "Inner Circles are idea *incubators."* They go on to explain that "Inner Circle members can be like 'angels.'" And that "Investors in a Broadway play in New York have long been referred to as 'angels.' Angels in your Inner Circle are people who 'invest' their resources—time, talents, ideas, and so on—to accomplish a specific task."

Here's a bit of what happened for us in just 18 months.

Through various opportunities to be critiqued, mentored in large and small groups, develop friendships one-on-one with various members of our group, and, of course, to be beneficiaries of Bob and Mark's direct wisdom, we began to see action. Dr. Joe Vitale would say we began to "attract" what we needed from our experience.

We published our first book for kids, called *I Wish I Knew What to Do?! ... Teens Tell It Like It Is ... On What to Do to Get Bullies to Leave You Alone.* By leveraging an introduction to Mark and Bob's publicist, we have been either featured or mentioned in *USA Today,* the *New York Post, People, Time,* and *CNN Headline News,* interviewed on numerous morning drive radio shows and talk radio show features across the country, and become subject matter experts on cyberbullying.

We've improved our company's sales focus with new sales directions, better salespeople, and innovative technology-based marketing tools introduced to us through our Inner Circle experience. For example, we met Allen Fahden, author of *Innovation on Demand* and *Is Half the World Crazy?,* and are coauthoring a book with him for our education niche. Our generous Inner Circle teammates gave freely of their time and expertise wherever possible. We've met countless people we would never have met through our own network, and so much more.

Even though we had taken our previous company public, we needed to learn new skills and create a new network that transcended our past, and we did that through our Inner Circle experience. You can, too.

Though we knew of Joe Vitale through Mark and Bob's larger network, our Inner Circle experience allowed us to speed up our "Attractor Factor" and bring back friends from a previous networking group who introduced us to Joe.

We close with what is absolutely the most important point and a character trait you must possess as a necessity with any mastermind, roundtable, or Inner Circle experience you pursue. It's called the Law of Reciprocity. You must *first* be willing to serve and pledge to never manifest scarcity but create and attract only abundance, of which you will be the first to share. Enrich others and you will enrich yourself.

To your Inner Circle success!

TWO IS ENOUGH

John J. O'Callaghan, author of *13 Home-Based Part-Time Money-Making Opportunities for Teenagers*

"Very dangerous," I thought, the first time I read about the mastermind group concept in Napoleon Hill's book, *Think and Grow Rich.*

As I recall, Hill said he practiced it by conjuring up the spirits of famous dead people (See Chapter 8, "The Imaginary Mastermind Group"), imagining he was seated in a roundtable conference with them, and asking them what they would do in a given situation.

I was 19 at the time. I grew up in Ireland and was raised on a diet of ghost stories and supernatural happenings that scared the "you know what" out of me. So, I read every book on occultism, spiritualism, and black magic I could get hold of, and as a direct result, I knew just why Hill's advice was very dangerous.

Years later, a colleague and I became good friends. Every day we talked about success, money, and power and shared not only our dreams, but our thoughts and ideas. He bounced his biz ideas off me and I bounced my ideas off him. We argued. If my argument was the most logical or likely, I won. If his was, he won.

That's when it struck me. We were using a live version Hill's mastermind concept and it worked like magic. We started a business as 50/50 partners and became very, very successful in a comparatively short time.

Subsequently we joined forces with three more partners. But that didn't work.

We lost money. Then we joined with two more partners. We made money but we were not happy and could hardly wait to sell our shares in a reverse buyout.

Although my original partner and I are no longer in business together—he is in the U.K. and I am in the United States—we talk on the phone every week and have lots of fun exchanging business ideas.

My conclusion is that although the mastermind concept works, the problem is that like-minded people and truly trustworthy people are as rare as hen's teeth!*

[* For John's two free reports, "Test Your Entrepreneurial I.Q." and "The Truth about Partners," send an e-mail to johnocallaghan29@comcast.net.]

10

COMMON QUESTIONS (WITH ANSWERS)

Teamwork is the ability to work together toward a common vision. The ability to direct individual accomplishments toward organizational objectives. It is the fuel that allows common people to attain uncommon results.

—Andrew Carnegie

Question: Where do I find like-minded people to start my mastermind group?

Answer: You can start right where you're sitting. You can do everything from attend other business groups, such as Rotary clubs, or church groups. You can join a few discussion lists online. You can run an ad in a local newspaper or online. You can start talking to people in line at the post office, just to see who's interested.

Question: How do you create an atmosphere for people to share their ideas without worrying about the ideas being taken by someone else?

Answer: Trust is a fundamental element of a good mastermind. Far too many people live in fear that their ideas will be stolen. The truth is, more ideas are never acted on because of this fear.

Question: Is it better to gather experts you don't know yet and use the sum of their existing knowledge, or share the learning experience with a group of existing friends who don't have the knowledge yet?

Answer People underestimate their own value and experience. No matter who you are, you have education and experience that others don't have. Your view of the world, your way of working and living, will be different. As a result, your contribution is priceless. It's the same with anyone who attends a mastermind. A gardener may have thoughts that shake you awake. You may have ideas that awaken the gardener. Don't focus on "experts," as everyone is an expert in some way, in some area.

Question What is the purpose of the group?

Answer: That's up to you. You decide it when you plan it. It should be focused on one result: to achieve a goal, finish a project, or create something in your business or the community or what have you. Again, the world is yours.

Question: Will I be able to give enough so that I can get enough?

Answer: This is really a self-esteem question. Each person has unique contributions. You can invite a 5-year-old to your mastermind and, despite his or her limited education and experience, you will benefit from a view that is different from yours. That 5-year-old may say or do something that inspires you to reach your goal. The point is, everyone has something to offer.

Question: What sort of confidentiality/nondisclosure agreements are appropriate for a mastermind group?

Answer: None. It's usually considered insulting to ask people to sign a nondisclosure agreement, as it says you don't trust them. But this is your group. If you think all members would feel better signing a legal agreement of secrecy, then act on it.

Question: Once you have your group together, what is the best way to stay focused on your goals?

Answer If it's a goal you want, it should be easy to stay focused on it. This is a little like asking, "If I don't want to quit smoking, how do I quit?" A mastermind whose members are not interested in an agreed goal will not last. Again, the purpose of your group needs to be stated right up front, when you invite people to join.

Question: Who will be the facilitator, and what training/skills are required?

Answer: You can be the leader, and no training is needed. Remember, you aren't teaching anything in a mastermind; you are sharing and supporting each other to achieve an agreed on goal. For more on facilitating, see Chapter 14.

Question: I have been invited to join a few mastermind groups, but the rules and formalities have always put me off. Are all the rules really necessary, or would an informal "meeting of minds" for brainstorming sessions work just as well?

Answer: Your mastermind group doesn't need a set of rules as much as an agreed on structure. That's it. You can certainly have a meeting that is brainstorming only, but unless you have at least a time (duration) structure, the group may get out of hand or go off topic.

Question: How do you decide on a specific focus for the hour or session, and how do you gracefully give everybody equal time?

Answer: Some groups select topics in advance to focus on for a particular session; others don't. One of the things your group could do early on is brainstorm a list of topics or themes to discuss in meetings. However, it's not necessary to have a theme for each meeting. In the Wimberley Group, each member sets the agenda for his or her turn. We have a set amount of time for each member. In our group, it's 20 minutes. Some groups allow only 10 to 15 minutes per member. We recommend using a digital timer to keep track of the time. A small kitchen timer with an alarm is good for this, as an alarm sounds when time is up. We use the digital hourglass made by Polder. It's under $20 and can be found online at www.SkyMall.com.

Question: I tend to hide behind my computer, and I have always had a belief that one of the important components of a mastermind group is meeting in person. How important is meeting in person? Can you get the same benefit from a web conference, e-mail, or teleconference mastermind, or is there some dynamic of an in-person mastermind that makes it a priority?

Answer: As Internet marketers and authors, we spend a lot of time behind the computer ourselves. Our weekly mastermind meetings allow us to get outside the house for a few hours and interact with others face-to-face. For people who work in large offices or in a retail setting, the social aspect may be less important.

Advantages to face-to-face meetings include being able to pass around handouts, product samples, and sales copy. Cross talk is a lot easier to manage while brainstorming in a mastermind group when you can clearly see who's saying what.

The primary disadvantages include time, finding a satisfactory meeting place, and finding members in your area. People meeting online or by phone don't have to commute to or from a meeting location. They can also mastermind with people outside their local area. That makes it easier to find enough members to form a solid group. It also opens up the possibilities of masterminding with people in your own industry without worrying about competition. For example, a guitar shop owner in San Diego can form a group with guitar shop owners in, say, Atlanta, Philadelphia, Manchester, Paris, and Sydney without worrying about someone stealing his competition in his local market.

Question: Does everyone have to be a success already? How do you set up a group when you haven't made any money yet?

Answer: You don't have to already be successful to start a mastermind group. A group of beginners can enjoy the same benefits from a mastermind group as a person with 20 years of experience. Even a group of five or six complete novices has a much greater chance of success than someone trying to succeed alone. Regardless of experience, people in a mastermind can take advantage of having accountability partners, shared research and resources, and the ability to brainstorm and get feedback on their ideas.

Question: How do you handle the less than positive person who gets in the group?

Answer: Here an ounce of prevention is worth a pound of cure. The best way to avoid having negative people in your group is to carefully interview them before they join. Another way to control this is by bringing in members on a trial basis. After three or four meetings, or whatever interval you agree on, the group votes on whether to allow the new person to become a permanent member. The group should also agree, in advance, on the ground rules for your group and what to do if any member becomes problematic. That may involve calling for a vote, or it may be left up to the leader to decide.

Despite these precautions, if you still end up with that "less than positive person," the first thing to do is have the leader speak to the person privately about his or her attitude. If that doesn't work and the behavior continues, "fire" the person according to whatever ground rules you set up initially for your group. If you allow the negative behavior to continue, it will disrupt the harmony in your group. When harmony is gone, so is productivity. Nip problems like this in the bud.

Question: How is setting up a mastermind group different from networking in the traditional sense, and how do you select suitable, willing, cooperative people?

Answer: For one thing, mastermind groups tend to be much smaller than networking groups. In a networking group, you might interact heavily with some members while barely getting to know others. In a mastermind group, you'll work closely with and get to know each member well. A lot more trust is involved in a mastermind group than in a networking group.

See Chapters 4 and 5 for details on how to select suitable members for your mastermind group.

Question: Overwhelmed! (1) I have a full-time therapy practice and am already combating a number of pulls on my time (e-mail, courses, coaches, teleseminars, etc.), which have in many cases inter-fered with getting my e-business going. How can I add one more thing and what would I have to drop? (2) I live in an isolated area and have pondered for two years who I might approach. The only names I have come up with are former clients, and working with them would present an ethical breach. (3) That leaves the Internet. I know various Internet marketers, but haven't met any who I think really understand the minefield that someone in a regulated profession like psychology has to walk in. I know lots of other psychologists, but none who will admit an interest in or knowledge of marketing. Where should I start?

Answer: We know how difficult time management can be for the self-employed, especially in an Internet marketing business. Giving up an entire afternoon once a week for mastermind meetings isn't always easy. However, the returns on that time investment are tremendous and worth finding a way to make it happen.

As for finding members in your own backyard, sometimes you'll be amazed at who you might find. We live in Wimberley, Texas, a town of only about 5,000 people. Yet we've been able to build a very effective local group.

If you've been looking for two years and still haven't found someone, we'd suggest either taking your search online or considering a group where the other members are in different industries. If you can't find other psychologists, consider doctors, dentists, attorneys, financial planners, accountants, and other professionals in industries with similar regulatory restrictions.

In addition to your local chamber of commerce, you should pay particular attention to which of these professionals is advertising in the local paper or telephone directory. Also, note if any of these people are writing a column in the local paper or newsweekly. People paying for advertising or writing articles are interested in marketing.

Finally, if you need help getting control of your time, I (Bill) recommend reading David Allen's excellent book, *Getting Things Done: The Art of Stress-Free Productivity.* This is not your average time management book. I liked it so much I bought a copy for everyone in our mastermind group.

Question: Napoleon Hill's writing makes it clear that for best results, the members of my mastermind group should come from a higher stratum of success—both personal and financial—rather than from my peer group. If I want to be successful like Bill and Joe, how do I get them to be members of my mastermind?

Answer: People are often afraid to approach those at higher success levels. They assume that the more experienced person won't be interested in joining their group. This is a false assumption. With the Wimberley Group, we started with two complete newbies online and a best-selling author. If you're the one going to the trouble of putting the group together, you're making a contribution that has value to others. Successful people are often busy and will appreciate a situation where all they have to do is show up.

Question: Is a mastermind group the same as a support team for a business?

Answer: It can be. We call that type of group an advisory board mastermind. In this type of group, everyone has a specific role to play toward achieving a specific goal. The same could be said for the various support staff of a political candidate, a movie star, a celebrity athlete, or a recording artist. This would also include nonprofit and volunteer organizations working with fund-raising or to help with a particular cause.

However, it can also be a mutual support mastermind group. Each member is there to get support reaching personal goals while helping the other members pursue their own individual goals. The difference between the two kinds of groups is usually, but not always, common goals versus individual goals. Also, in the advisory board model, members are sometimes compensated for their efforts.

Question: Can the mastermind group be retired successful people from any walk of life?

Answer: Certainly. In fact, retired successful people can be the best type of mastermind members to have. These people have valuable experience to share, yet they don't have the busy schedule of active professionals. Retired people are often eager to share their experience and may be grateful for the opportunity to contribute.

Anyone who's had a lifetime of success in business, even if in a completely different industry from yours, will possess a wealth of knowledge that will benefit your mastermind. This is also the path to take if you'd like to form an advisory board mastermind but lack the resources to compensate your members. You may find retirees happy to participate without compensation, especially if it's a group that meets less frequently, say quarterly.

For this type of group, consider reserving a private room in a restaurant and picking up the tab for lunch for the group.

Question: Why should someone who would be valuable in a mastermind be interested in joining it when he or she has reached a level that I am only now trying to reach?

Answer: For one thing, many successful people remember what it was like starting out and enjoy helping others. Another reason is that you might possess a skill they don't. For example, you might be very good at working with computers. Many successful people are absolutely clueless when it comes to technology. So you have experience that's valuable to them even though they're more successful.

Also, many successful people would like to join a mastermind group but don't have the time or energy to put one together themselves. By being the person that organizes the group, you're providing a valuable service. Plus, once you get one successful person in your group, it's easier to get others to join.

Sure, some successful people will turn you down, but don't let that discourage you from asking others. Persistence usually pays off.

Question: What if you don't know five or six people whose opinions you value? I spend more time with newsletters of advisors I have selected than actual people. When Napoleon Hill identified the mastermind phenomenon there did not exist daily e-mail subscriptions from Dan Kennedy, Brian Tracey, Donald Trump, Robert Kiyosaki, Bob Baker, and Robert Allen. For all practical purposes, these are my mastermind group. You enroll them with a click of your mouse.

Answer: That's fine for feeding your brain with more information, but you don't get *any* interaction or *any* feedback that way. You also can't brainstorm or share projects with those e-zine writers. You're on your own, trying to be a lone ranger in a world that shoots solitary riders off their horse on a daily basis. As for not knowing six people you value, you might need to get out more. You're no more the smartest person in the world than we are. All the greats got feedback. If you really feel that you are the wisest person on earth, then join Mensa and enlist a few of them to be in your first mastermind.

PART II

Because no one person knows it all when it comes to masterminds, Joe and I invited a few experts to contribute their thoughts, ideas, and advice. You'll find their chapters in this section.

11

WHAT THE HECK IS GROUP DYNAMICS? And What Does It Have to Do with Masterminds?

Jillian Coleman Wheeler*

[* Jillian Coleman Wheeler began her career as a counselor to individuals, couples, families, and groups. For many years, she has been a funding and business consultant. Through her web sites, www.GrantMeRich.com and www.NewAmericanLandRush.com, she writes and teaches about achieving success in grant writing, business, and life.]

A favorite subject for psychologists and other folks who study human behavior is "group dynamics," a psychobabble term for the way people relate to each other in groups. In fact, hundreds of thousands of scholarly pages have been written on the subject.

It's not too surprising. After all, psychologists are human beings themselves. Each of them, and each of us, began life as part of a group: our family of origin. Every one of us, whether we were welcomed and cherished or our arrival was an unhappy surprise, had to find our own place in the family group. If a younger sibling followed us or an older sibling went off to college, if a parent left or a grandparent moved in, we had to struggle through the family shuffle and redefine our role.

As we got a little older and began to move outside the perimeter of our original family, we became members of other groups. We were one of the play-mates on the playground and one of the students in our class. We were part of a sports team, or a school band, or a science club.

Now that we're grown-ups, we are members of groups in our workplace and of the organizations we join. We feel our way to a comfortable place among our group of friends. And, of course, we form our own new families, either through marriage and par-enthood or through other close, enduring relation-ships.

So why are we, as members of a mastermind group, interested in what a bunch of psychologists and social scientists have to say about group dynam-ics?

Well, aside from groups' common human experi-ences, psychologists have another reason to find groups so fascinating. Years of observation have shown that all of us operate differently in groups than we do in solitary situations. Groups come together and take on lives of their own. In fact, a group is a separate entity, with its own power to shape and af-fect our behavior when we are together.

If we can understand this process, at least to some degree, we're more likely to have a successful mastermind group, and to enjoy the experience.

Here is another closely related psychological principle. Often, we aren't feeling what we're feeling for the reasons we think we're feeling the way we feel.

Did you get that?

It refers to the unconscious, a part of us that operates below the surface. Every emotion we feel in every event throughout our lives gets stored in our unconscious mind. Then, when we aren't paying attention, something happens in our present-day reality that triggers one of those old feelings. Our unconscious responses frequently affect our experience in life and in groups, including our mastermind groups.

Few people grow up without having at least some unpleasant group experiences. Maybe our family situations were painful, at least some of the time. Maybe we remember being left out when teams were chosen on the playground or the sports field. Some of us were teased by classmates, or even teachers, for being too smart, or not smart enough, or for being "different" in some way from the other kids. As grown-ups, most of us have dealt with office politics or the jockeying for position that always seems to be present, even in church and community organizations.

On the other hand, however, most of us have also experienced the positive power of groups. Anyone who has been part of a winning sports team, or a member of a math team, or an actor in a play, or participated in a food drive knows the pleasure of contributing to a group accomplishment. Groups allow us to learn from each other, support each other, and accomplish more together than any one of us might accomplish alone.

There are lots of different kinds of groups (in fact, any time two or more people are in each other's company, a group exists). Some of us have participated in therapy groups or consciousness-raising groups. Mastermind groups are considered "task groups." Task groups are formed to accomplish a certain body of work. In the case of the mastermind group, that purpose is usually to support the goals of the individual members. Those goals may be either business or personal, or a combination of the two. I have spent several years in two very different mastermind groups, and I think they are most effective when they allow members to request support in both areas of life.

Over the years, psychologists who specialize in studying group dynamics have developed many different ways of analyzing what happens among participants. One of those people is Bruce Tuckman, PhD, and his work gives us a simple framework for looking at groups.

Dr. Tuckman describes five phases in the development of a group:

1. Forming
2. Storming
3. Norming
4. Performing

5.   Adjourning

These phases of development do not necessarily happen in sequence. To some degree, they often overlap.

During the *forming* period, members are getting to know each other. When we join a group, we want to be accepted, so at this stage all the members usually avoid any controversy or conflict. On a deeper level, we are closely observing each other and forming conscious judgments and unconscious impressions. These deeper impressions will be very important as the group moves forward.

While the group is forming, not much actual work gets done. A good way for members to move quickly and successfully through this period is to use some introduction activities that help people connect with each other.

Next is the *storming* period. This is when the members begin to come into conflict. The conflict can be over any issue, but it's good to understand in advance that in groups, conflict is inevitable. It is guaranteed. This conflict may be out in the open, or it may take place below the surface. Frequently, the real issue is around who in the group will hold power and how differences will be resolved.

For those of us who are members or facilitators of mastermind groups, it can be helpful to understand several issues that come up during this period. The first is the issue of roles. By the time members join the mastermind group, they have generally settled into their most comfortable "group role." Some people are leaders, and depending on their experience and insight, some of the leaders may engage in a struggle for power.

More emotionally mature leaders will step forward to lead in some cases and allow others to lead when appropriate. Some people prefer to be followers, but everyone in the group wants to understand what his or her contribution will be and to be valued as an important member.

Another issue is "transference." Transference is a psychological term that describes the process of unconsciously relating to another person as though that person were someone in our past. Here are two simple examples. If you are a woman who had a dominating father you struggled to escape, or a domineering husband you managed to leave in your past, you may have a hard time dealing with a group member who is a strong male leader. It may be hard to see him as a separate personality with his own particular good qualities. Or you may be a man who finds that another member reminds you of an old girlfriend who was manipulative in your relationship. It will be difficult for you to sort out your unconscious response to this person from the present reality.

Transference is a real phenomenon, and it takes place all the time in all our life situations. Struggles for power happen all the time, too, often very politely. A lot of the time, we remain largely unconscious of these processes. But because groups—all kinds of groups—re-create for us our family of origin, they tend to bring every issue to the forefront in a very powerful way. One very helpful way to avoid tumult during the storming period is to agree on the group structure, roles, and expectations early on.

Sometimes we enter the mastermind group with preexisting relationships. Sometimes two members become friends outside the group. At times, the men in a group may naturally treat each other differently than they treat the women, and the women may feel excluded. At other times, the women in a group may identify with one another, and the men may feel excluded. It's important to hold the mastermind meeting as a sort of "sacred space," where everyone is equal and included.

During the *norming* stage, the discord settles down. At this point, we as members are clear about the structure, goals, and tasks of the group, and we have a good idea of our own part in the group process. We have come to appreciate each other and feel genuinely supportive of each other. We're willing to put aside previous judgments. At this stage, the productive work of the group really begins.

Two things must be remembered about the norming stage. First, if there is any confusion about the structure and operation of the group, we as members will feel off balance and uncomfortable. For example, if some members of the group are consistently late or miss meetings, these issues need to be addressed. If the group is going to function smoothly, the structure must be absolutely understood and agreed on by everyone, and everyone must actively buy in to the operating guidelines.

Second, we need to remember that the group has worked very hard to reach this current level of accord, and it is important to understand that any change will feel threatening to the members. For this reason, any decision, such as changing time or place, the format of the group, or accepting new members, needs to be discussed openly. For the group to remain happy and effective, every member must buy in to the change. Also, if new members are accepted, the group will redo the earlier stages, and that is an important reality to consider as membership decisions are made.

During the *performing* stage, the group is functioning well, and members feel at home and productive. We as group members depend on each other and are secure enough to be flexible. Members flow easily in and out of their roles, according to the needs of the group. There is a feeling of belonging, pride, and loyalty to the group. Because of the high level of comfort experienced in the group, members suddenly find they can accomplish great things. Nevertheless, at times the group will fall back into a storming phase, and members will be challenged to resolve new issues.

Eventually, every mastermind group will dissolve, and this is called the *adjourning* stage. The decision to end the group is difficult because it involves change and loss. Depending on our own individual experiences, this stage can bring up unresolved feelings of loss and grief from earlier in life. Group members are often surprised to find how sad they feel and may even want to deny the feeling. It is important to acknowledge and respect the adjourning process and to talk about it openly. It is often helpful to have some ceremony celebrating the accomplishments of the group.

One of the foundations of group dynamics is the idea that we are all moving forward and improving our ability to have satisfying relationships. If we were lucky enough to come from a family where communication was open, honest, clear, and compassionate, we start life with an enormous advantage (psychologists estimate that no more than 20 percent of people grow up in highly functional families). The rest of us learn as we move through life. Participation in a mastermind group is an opportunity for us to grow as individuals and lovingly support our fellow members in their growth.

When we as members of the mastermind group understand group dynamics and pay attention to what's happening under the surface, at the unconscious level, we have the very best opportunity to reach the performing stage and achieve our individual and group goals. We also maximize our chances of success when group members reach early agreement and clarity about goals, structure, rules, and roles and when we agree to treat each other with understanding, tolerance, kindness, and honesty.

12

SELECTING THE RIGHT PEOPLE FOR YOUR MASTERMIND GROUP

Michael Licenblat*

[* Michael Licenblat, BSc (Psychology) is a resilience expert who helps people in business bounce back fast from pressure, stress, and burnout in their work and life. He is a professional speaker, coach, and author. Find out more about Michael at www.BounceBackFast.com.]

When you run your business by yourself, it is easy to become sidetracked, lose interest in a project, feel overwhelmed by the workload, or even give up altogether. At times, everything can feel too hard and like you'll never get there, or that there is just too much to do.

In this frame of mind, your energy becomes quickly drained, your mind is easily distracted, and you become less effective in driving your business.

In 1976, psychologists Maier and Seligman conducted experiments, finding that when dogs felt that they were unable to escape from a pain, they gave up trying and just whimpered. This state is known as *learned helplessness.* Although this experiment was very cruel, this state of learned helplessness has also been identified in people.

When people believe that their efforts cannot change or influence their destiny, they develop a sense of helplessness and powerlessness. Feeling helpless, overwhelmed, or stressed reduces the amount of effort and perseverance you put into pursuing your goals and also drains your motivation.

One key factor in overcoming helplessness or the feeling of being overwhelmed is having a sense of support from other people in a microcommunity where you are not alone.

A mastermind group is a supportive group of like-minded people who collectively brainstorm ideas, strategies, techniques, and concepts to help each other move forward in their business and life and become unstuck.

A mastermind group is not a social gathering of friends, neither is it a session to air your complaints about life and feel sorry for yourself. To make a mastermind group work, it has to be made up of people who are positive, self-motivated, and proactive and who have a desire to help others reach their goals.

The selection of the right people is critical to the success of your mastermind group. Here are some criteria to consider.

1. SELECT DOERS, NOT TALKERS

It is of little value to be in a group of people who talk about what needs to be done or things they could do and not to take action on them. This creates inertia. That is, it reinforces your feeling of "stuckness" because no change is being put in place.

Instead, ensure that people have a track record of results, that they actually do what it is they say they will do—and not just talk about it. If it is just the company that you enjoy, then get a dog.

2. SELECT BITERS, NOT LEECHES

In the insect world, a biter confronts and attacks by striking, whereas a leech sucks its victim dry.

In mastermind groups, it is better to have biters. These are people who offer honest, upfront, and direct feedback on your work by giving you information and insight that is of value. Biters are good communicators and openly share their wisdom and time with others in the group.

Leeches are takers. They sit and suck in information and tips from others, offering very little value to the group. They are often insecure people who have a working attitude of taking instead of sharing and giving. Leeches are often overfriendly—until they get what they want and then drop you like a hot potato.

3. SELECT DRIVERS, NOT DRAGGERS

Drivers take initiative; they set goals and action plans and inspire others to step up a level and become all they can be. They believe in themselves and push others to excel. They are forward focused and spend little, if any, time worrying about the past or wallowing in their mistakes.

Draggers don't lead, they follow the herd. They don't express their opinion unless asked. They have to be encouraged to try new things and often resist change. They drag back the progress of the others in the group because they are waiting for someone to give them the answer instead of being proactive in finding it themselves.

13

MANAGING YOUR MEETING MONSTERS Identifying the Cast of Culprits Who Threaten Productive Meetings

Craig Harrison*

[* Craig Harrison is a professional speaker, corporate trainer, and communication consultant who builds stellar sales and service organizations and credible communicators. You can reach Craig through his web site: www.ExpressionsOfExcellence.com, e-mail: solutions@craigspeaks.com, or call him toll-free at (888)450-0664.]

In the famous *Star Wars* bar scene, patrons knew, by appearance, what type of zany character was sitting beside them. Each character had a distinctive look. Yet in meetings, you may have no idea about the constellation of characters you're meeting with. That's because their normal outward appearances belie often troublesome behavior. Use this chapter as your guide to the crazy cast of characters you're likely to encounter in your meetings. Whether or not you're armed with a light saber, you'll nevertheless be equipped to do battle with these often destructive forces who subvert meetings with their bothersome behavior.

THE MONOPOLIZER

This person thinks he or she is the only one with wisdom on any subject.

Monopolizers believe everyone else is there to hear them speak, and so they do, incessantly. They don't appreciate that meetings offer an opportunity to hear from many.

They prattle on and on, arrogantly acting as though their ideas or beliefs are inherently more important than others'. Sadly, other people shy away from contributing, intimidated by the monopolizer's stranglehold on the meeting. When facilitators allow this, it sends a message that their rudeness is sanctioned. *The facilitator, or even other meeting participants, should indicate an interest in hearing from others in the meeting to remind the monopolizer that others can speak as well as listen.*

THE TANGENT TALKER

This person hijacks the topic of the group by taking discussions off on tangents—topics unrelated to the issue at hand. One minute you're on topic and the next minute you're in left field as your agenda topic disappears in a tangent.

Your meeting chair's ability to recognize and refocus is essential to a productive meeting. "Let's remember to confine ourselves to the topic at hand" is a good way to get back on track. As an alternative, saying "Let's try to avoid tangents" also labels such behavior as contrary to the group's aims. As well, you can "park" extraneous items in a "parking lot" list, where they're noted, if only to be addressed later.

THE DEVIL'S ADVOCATE

Let's face it, there's one in every crowd and most meetings, too. This person seems to relish taking the opposite tack. Whatever the argument being put forth, this person delights in taking an opposing view. It's sport for him, an exercise in opposition. The more unpopular the stance, the more exciting the challenge. Often he begins by saying, "Just for the sake of argument ... I believe the opposite is true." Though there's value in looking at issues from multiple points of view and avoiding groupthink, the Devil's Advocate applies the technique to every issue, every argument, and every conversation. Hold on to your agenda and get comfortable. This could take a while!

A good chair can praise this person's ability to do this while simultaneously indicating its inappropriateness given time parameters or previously agreed on issues.

THE CYNIC

The ultimate naysayer, cynics have a master's degree in negativity. Adroit at the phrase "It won't work," they are skilled at deflating and defeating whatever motion is in motion. "Can't be done." "They'll never buy it." "We tried it once and it was a failure." Their motto: Just say no.

Challenge these people to think like the Devil's Advocate and suppose that things could work. Use the common conflict resolution tool of asking them to embrace the other side's view as if it were their own and argue that side's position.

THE FENCE SITTER

Known for their paralysis by analysis, these characters are unable to make decisions. Despite being in a deliberative body, they are conflicted by multiple arguments and can't pull the trigger when it's time to make a decision in a meeting.

They provide fodder for the Devil's Advocate, the Cynic, and other characters with their ambivalence. Whether they are afraid of being wrong, of disagreeing with someone, or of just going on record, they are a meeting monster for their inability to move the action forward.

Try to cajole them to action. Remind them they have a vote and were invited to use it. Ask them their opinions on matters to draw them out and get them on record.

THE BROWN NOSER

There's likely one in every meeting: the person who is so obsequious, bending over backward to ingratiate himself or herself to the boss, the meeting leader, or other power broker. Brown Nosers are so busy currying favor with others that they subvert whatever true feelings they have about issues to kiss butt. They are seen to be in the pocket of the person they're kowtowing to. Ultimately they are seen for who they are and become predictable.

Try to elicit their ideas and preferences before asking others as a way of drawing them out.

THE PANDORA'S BOX OPENER

These meeting monsters just have to tackle issues that are emotional, touchy, or hot buttons for others in the meeting. In every meeting there are topics sure to strike a nerve, to provoke an emotional reaction, or to throw the group into a quagmire. These people lead the entire meeting into areas that provoke frustration, animosities, and often resentment. Once this box is opened, it's hard to get its issues back inside. Discussions of salaries, promotions, or personal styles often stir up issues that hijack meetings. Even worse, some culprits reopen issues from earlier in the meeting that have already been resolved.

The best cure: a firm "Let's not go there" from the meeting's facilitator. Other phrases, such as "Let's cross that bridge when we get to it" or "That's a hornets' nest we don't need to disturb," label certain subjects out of bounds.

THE ATTACKER

As children, these people were bullies. Some haven't grown up! The attacker deftly mixes negativity with personal attacks, challenging others' ideas with vigor. Without regard to hurting others' feelings, attackers use a confrontational style to object to others' ideas and go against the flow. Sadly, sometimes they don't even realize they're attacking.

A good facilitator can refocus them to be positive, to remove the sting from their words, and avoid an adversarial approach. All meeting participants are entitled to stop the meeting when attacked personally. People can criticize your actions or beliefs, but you don't have to tolerate attacks against who you are as a person.

THE JOKER

Don't let their good nature fool you, Jokers can be meeting monsters. Their constant joking has the effect of diminishing others' serious ideas or suggestions. Their infusion of humor can belittle others' motions and makes it difficult for some to be taken seriously. There is a time and place for joking. We all like a good laugh, but constant joking disrupts a meeting and distracts attention from where it should be.

A meeting chair can designate several minutes at the start or middle of a meeting specifically for humor. When it crops up elsewhere and is deemed disruptive, the chair can remind people that the time for humor has passed or is forthcoming, so as to control it.

THE ROBOTS

These meeting monsters are actually cell phones, pagers, personal digital assistants (PDAs), and laptops. They distract their owner and others as they intrude on participants' attention during meetings. It's gotten so bad now that cell phones contain cameras within them—just what meetings need.

A good meeting chair will create ground rules for meetings, including turning off these gadgets at the outset. It's hard to compete with human distractions, let alone electronic ones as well.

As you can see, meetings are full of characters. You should study the behavior in meetings, including your own, to better understand your style of interaction. The character of your meeting will surely be affected by the characters in your meeting.

May the force be with you.

14

10 TIPS FOR FACILITATING MASTERMIND GROUP MEETINGS

Karyn Greenstreet, Passion For Business, LLC (www.passionforbusiness.com)

Here are 10 tips for keeping your mastermind group running smoothly:

1. *It's all about democracy.* Consider using the very first mastermind meeting to discuss all group rules and take a vote on them. Let your group make its own decisions about how the group is structured, the number of people in the group, when it will meet and for how long, what the theme or focus of the group will be, what topics are permissible or out of bounds, and whether a new member can join. Members should decide on the rules of how the group works together—and what the punishments are for not following these rules. Members should also decide on the tone of the group: casual, feet to the fire, or somewhere in between. In this way, the group decides how to meet its own needs.

2. *Play the appropriate role.* Decide if you are a facilitator or a member, or both, and act accordingly. If you are simply the facilitator, then you don't get a vote in group decisions unless the decision directly affects you (e.g., the time or location of the meetings). As a facilitator, your sole job is to keep the meetings, and the group administration, going forward. Even if you are an expert in the field that is the theme of the group, your voice should always be heard last, to give the members a chance to mastermind among themselves. Otherwise, members may look to you as the guru, and all cross-member masterminding will come to a grinding halt.

3. *Make the meeting a safe place.* Attending mastermind group meetings is a very deep and personal experience, and over time, as rapport builds, members will want to share some very private information about themselves. As the facilitator, it is your job to create a space in each meeting where members feel safe in expressing their true selves, their hopes and fears, and the real things that are happening in their lives. When members do share difficult personal thoughts and feelings, give them room to express themselves and verbally tell them it's okay to share in this way. (However, be on alert for members who consistently use meetings as a psychotherapy session. If they repeatedly bring emotional problems to the group but never take action to move forward,

gently take them aside and explain the rules.) Remind members that this is a confidential space, and discussing other members' situations is not allowed outside the meetings. If necessary, ask members to sign a confidentiality agreement, especially if they're talking about ideas that could be patented, trademarked, or copyrighted.

4. *Have a structure.* It's a good idea to have meetings on the same day and hour each week or month so that people can block out that time in their appointment book. Have a structure of how each meeting will progress. In our groups, the formula is this: open the meeting, share success stories, mastermind time, share resources, close the meeting. The largest portion of time should be for the mastermind time, when members take turns sharing their goals and challenges and everyone asks questions and gives advice to that member. This keeps the meeting from deteriorating into a chatty social session. Should the discussion become social, steer the meeting back to its structure. Some mastermind groups work from a book, selecting a chapter or exercise to work on in each session, which helps to establish a structure.

5. *Keep track of time.* Use a timer with an audible buzzer to ensure that everyone gets an equal amount of mastermind time. Typically, 10 to 15 minutes per member should be sufficient. Members who are in crisis can request extra time from

the group, and the group can vote whether to give that member the extra time. If extra time is given, then another member must volunteer to give up some of his or her time so that the meeting doesn't drag on indefinitely.

6. *Use a talking stick.* Decide in advance the order in which members will speak at each meeting. In my groups, we rotate, so that each member gets to be the first speaker once in a while. For instance, if it's Pamela, Kat, Susan, Jamie, then Karyn in week one, we rotate and Kat goes first in week two, Susan goes first in week three, and so on. Then, when it's each member's time to talk, she has the floor exclusively and no one can interrupt until she is finished sharing. Members often find instant clarity through verbalizing their situation and thoughts, and it's imperative that this time be honored with silence from the others. In live meetings, you might actually want to have a talking stick, or some other object, that the member holds to show a sense of ownership and power of the time he or she has been allotted.

7. *Keep the conversation going, when appropriate.* As with any group discussion, there are normal quiet times when members are processing information or thinking of new ideas. These thinking times need to be honored with silence. As you learn to facilitate meetings, you will be able to discern this quiet thinking time from the awkward "I don't know what to say next" time. (Awkward

times will show themselves as people shifting in their seats or not making eye contact.) During awkward pauses, be prepared to jump into the discussion by asking a question or moving to another topic. If you use an online message board as part of your group communication, precreate some conversation starter questions so that when things get quiet on the message board, you're ready with a thought-provoking question.

8. *Goal keepers needed.* One of the hallmarks of mastermind groups is that members share their goals each month. Keep a record of these; goals help members find clarity, focus, and potential. Read them back to the group at the next meeting and ask members if they've achieved their stated goals. This creates a sense of integrity and accountability by reminding members that they are committed to completing a goal if they voice it.

9. *Discipline where needed.* Sometimes, members hog time even after the buzzer rings. At other times, one member may shoot down another member's ideas during brainstorming sessions. Members might show up late, or not show up at all. Members might voice goals and constantly miss achieving them each month. These types of members must be reminded that the purpose of your mastermind group is to help people achieve their potential and to help each other work through challenges and decisions in a balanced and democratic fashion. Don't let small problems

like these go unremarked. Pull the offending member aside and remind him or her of the rules.

10. *Be ready to fire a member.* If the situation gets too bad, you have to be ready to fire a member from the group. It's best if this is voted on by the group and if the group has a chance to air its grievance with the offending member. If the offending member is not present (perhaps he or she hasn't been to the past three meetings and hasn't been reachable by phone), it's still a good idea to discuss the situation openly with the group and reach a decision about what to do with the offending member. Note, however, that this type of discussion can eat into your masterminding time, so it may be best to have a separate meeting, or perhaps a teleconference, to discuss this administrative situation. As the facilitator, it is your job to communicate the group's vote to the offending member.

15

THE TRUTH ABOUT MASTERMINDS

Bill Harris (www.centerpointe.com)

There is a way to get all the knowledge, expertise, and connections you need to achieve your goal, and I want to tell you what it is right now. Napoleon Hill found that every successful person he ever met had what is called a mastermind group, which he described as an alliance of two or more minds working in perfect harmony for the attainment of a definite objective.

I've seen two kinds of mastermind groups. The first is the type Hill describes, where all the members are focused on the attainment of the same objective. Andrew Carnegie, Henry Ford, Thomas Edison—and, really, all great achievers—have had such a group, consisting of their management team, other related experts such as attorneys and accountants, and any other people who had specialized knowledge they needed.

In this kind of mastermind group, the originator of the group, the driving force behind the goal, gathers together a group of people who have the knowledge, expertise, and connections he or she lacks. My mastermind group includes experts in technology, operations, marketing, business law, and accounting, plus a number of other people who are experts at dealing with details and other tasks I'm not good at or don't want to do. These people collaborate to figure out how to achieve the goals of the business, often meeting to brainstorm, identify challenges and solve them, and otherwise figure out how to make the business go where I want it to go. A mastermind group is a practical way for you to appropriate and use the experience, training, education, specialized knowledge, and native intelligence of other people, as completely as if it were your own.

If your goal isn't a business, you can still have a mastermind group. An athlete may have a coach and a trainer, for instance. He or she might have a massage therapist and a dietician, an agent and an attorney. Pilots have an instructor and a mechanic, and the air traffic controllers are really part of their mastermind group while they are flying. If your goal is to travel around the world, your mastermind group might include a travel agent and the authors of many travel books, even though you might never actually meet them. Anyone whose ideas you pull into your decision-making process can be considered part of your mastermind group.

The second kind of mastermind group is where people with many different goals come together to support each other in the achievement of their goals. Although the people in this kind of group are not totally focused on your project all the time, they help you brainstorm and strategize and introduce you to other people and resources that might help you—and you do the same for them.

A mastermind group solves the problem of how to get the expertise, experience, resources, and specialized knowledge you don't have yourself. And guess what: There is a price to pay. If people are to join your mastermind group, there must be something in it for them. You might pay them, you might share the results of what you achieve together, or in some cases they might help you because they are already very successful and want to help someone else on the way up. They might help you because you are helping them. One way or another, though, there has to be something in it for them, and your job as the creator of the group is to make sure that the other members are generously compensated in one way or another.

If you're not sure how to do this, ask yourself the magic question: How will I make this mastermind group of great benefit to anyone who joins it? Keep asking until you figure out an answer. Here's a hint: Ask them what they want. Ask them what you can do for them. Find out what their deepest desires are, both materially and emotionally, and figure out a way for them to get what they want while you get what you want.

There are several keys to a good mastermind group. First, the group must share a definite purpose. Even if you have the second kind of group, where people with different goals come together to help each other, when you are discussing one person's goal, everyone must be focused in that moment on helping that person get what he or she wants, to the best of their ability. I belong to such a group, called the Transformational Leadership Council, which was started by Jack Canfield. This group contains 35 key personal growth leaders, and part of the group's purpose is to help each other achieve our goals. When my goals are the subject of the group, they all focus on how they can help me. When someone else is the subject, we all focus on helping that person.

Something extraordinary happens when you get two or more people together to focus on the same outcome. In such a case, one plus one is three, or even four, in terms of the power generated. Napoleon Hill noticed in his study of successful people that when two or more people coordinate their thinking through a mastermind alliance, they dramatically increase the ability to tap into what he called "Infinite Intelligence," and what I have referred to as that part of you that always knows exactly what to do. Ideas flow and problems seem to be easily solved.

Another crucial element in a mastermind alliance is harmony. There must be a complete meeting of the minds, without reservation on the part of any member. In a great mastermind alliance, each member subordinates his or her personal needs to the needs of the overall outcome or goal. If at any time the harmony of the group is damaged, you must immediately do something to restore it, including asking a member to leave, if that becomes necessary. A mastermind alliance cannot succeed if there is a lack of harmony. Never try to operate a mastermind alliance that includes negative people. And don't try it if you yourself are temporarily negative—though I realize that by now that probably isn't going to happen.

It also must be clear to each person how he or she will benefit from the group and what the contribution of each person will be. I suggest that you err on the side of generosity with the members of your mastermind group. And it is crucially important that the group share a single, definite purpose and that everyone be clear as to what that purpose is.

Quite often I see people bring in a mastermind partner whose sole qualification is being a friend or relative. Friends or relatives might make good mastermind partners, but they often don't. Choose the people in your mastermind group because of the expertise they bring to the table, not because they live next door, they are related to you, or you like them. This is how people get involved with what I call "the partner from Hell." Certainly don't bring in a mastermind partner just because you feel unsure of yourself and want some moral support. If you're unsure of yourself and bring in another person who is also unsure of himself or herself, you'll have a case of the blind leading the blind. Decide what expertise or resources you need and look for people who have it. And become sure of yourself, which you can do by focusing your mind on what you want.

If you need money for your goal, which is a common problem, one choice is to bring in someone who is interested in profiting from your goal and who has some money to invest. You put up the idea and the hard work, and your partner puts up the finances. Be careful, though, that you maintain harmony in your group. Part of that is being very clear up front regarding what is expected from each person and how each person will share in the rewards of the group. Also, beware of the fact that the person putting up the money might disagree with your plans but knows little or nothing about how to achieve the goal. Investors are notorious for butting in and making it difficult for entrepreneurs to do things the way they want to do them.

So, before you decide to start such a group, think about what you need and what you have to offer. Part of the process is knowing where you are and knowing where you want to be. I suggest you take a personal inventory of your assets and liabilities so you'll know what to look for as you put your mastermind group together, and so you'll know what you can offer the other members.

When I first started my group, I didn't have much confidence that I had a lot to offer anyone else, or that they would want to support what I wanted to do. And, because I had no money, I couldn't pay anyone. You may feel this way, too. But don't let that stop you from creating such a group. You'll be surprised at who will help if you ask. The first person I asked was a marketing expert, and the person who gave me his phone number told me he probably wouldn't even talk to me. But he did agree to see me at his office, and when I told him what I wanted to do, for some reason he took a liking to me and helped me. He even cut his fee in half. I'm not sure why, but I like to think that he saw my enthusiasm and sincerity, which came from my clear focus on my goal.

Certainly the people you would pay as you need them, such as an attorney or an accountant, are going to be willing to be a part of your group, and it's always possible to get some other people together who have similar goals, as Jack Canfield has done in creating the Transformational Leadership Council. As with anything else, take the first step, notice what happens, refine your strategy, and keep going. You'll be surprised at how easy it is to create such a group. Figure out what's in it for the other person, whether it's making money, being challenged, learning new things, helping others, or any other benefit. If you're starting a group of people who all have a business or at least the same general interest and you're getting together to brainstorm and share ideas, most people are eager to be in such a group.

Be sure, though, that you maintain harmony in your group, that the group agrees on a central purpose, and that you always keep in mind the benefit each member will receive—and do everything you can to be sure that all members receive those benefits. If you do this, you'll find that such a group is a fountain of ideas, and you'll have a much easier time getting the resources you need to achieve your goal.

Here's another way to look at a mastermind group, an idea I got from Dan Sullivan of The Strategic Coach. You have certain unique abilities, while lacking other abilities you might need to achieve your goal. This is why I wanted you to take an inventory or what you already have and what you need. What you're trying to do is to create a unique ability team. Now let me define the term "unique ability." A unique ability is something you're really good at and, at the same time, you are energized by doing it. Teaching is one of my unique abilities, and I'm energized by doing it. On the other hand, I'm good at managing people, but I don't really feel energized by doing it. In fact, I don't like it very much at all.

Ultimately, you want to be using your unique ability and delegating everything else to other people who have other unique abilities you need. This means that group members are doing what they are really good at and what energizes them. This makes for a very happy and productive group. What you don't want is for you or anyone else to be doing something you aren't very good at or, even if you are good at it, you don't like doing.

So you want to become clear about what your unique abilities are and also what unique abilities you need but don't have. You might be really good at strategizing, or be really good at implementing strategies created by others, or you might be really good at dealing with details, or really good with technology, or really good at negotiating, or really good at working with your hands, or really good at seeing relationships others don't notice. Begin to think about what your unique ability might be.

A big clue is to consider what energizes you. If you're good at it and it energizes you, it is a unique ability. If you're really good at it but you don't like doing it, it isn't a unique ability. Now, admittedly, in the beginning you may have to do everything regarding your goal. That's the way it is for most people. It certainly was for me, and I had to overcome the feeling I had of "Who would want to help *me,* or work with *me?"* Now it seems like everyone wants to work with me and help me. The feeling I had wasn't true—as is the case with many, if not all, bad feelings.

Once you know what your unique ability is, you can begin to think about creating a unique ability team. To do this, figure out what other unique abilities you need and look for people who have them. I, for instance, am not very good with details. If I force myself, I can be, but I don't like dealing with them if I can avoid it. I'm more of a big picture person. But I have several people who work for me who are geniuses when it comes to handling details and spotting mistakes in the details, and because that is their unique ability, they play an important role at Centerpointe.*

[* Over 160,000 people in 172 countries have worked with Centerpointe to make dramatic improvements in their lives. For a free demo CD of their Holosync technology, visit www.Centerpointe.com.]

Other people who work for me are good at organizing events, or good at managing other people, or good at technology, or good at implementing and managing projects. Now you might think that your unique abilities can't make you any money. Consider a few examples, though. Let's say you love to sit around and chat with people, and you're really good at it. "So what?" you say. "Who would pay me to do that?" Well, Oprah Winfrey makes $50 million a year doing just that. Jack Canfield told me about a friend who is an international tour director and makes a good living hanging out with people in some of the most exciting cities of the world. Rick Steeves likes to travel and to write about it. Over the past 20 years he has written many travel books, helping people travel on a limited budget but still have incredibly exciting vacations. He gets to travel all over the world to update his books.

Here's another example. Consider a woman whose main passion is watching soap operas. Now who would pay you to do that?! This woman discovered that many other people also love to watch soap operas but often miss their favorite shows for various reasons. So she created a magazine called *Soap Opera Digest.* Her job is to watch soap operas and write summaries of the plots for those who miss their favorite shows.

This is the kind of idea that comes from focusing on what you want and asking the magic "How can I?" question. So find out what you are uniquely good at and what you love to do, and ask yourself how you can create something where you get to do what you love. Then look for people with unique abilities that you need but don't have.

THE INNER COUNSEL THINK TANK The Mastermind Group That Advises You from Within!

Peter C. Siegel*

[* Peter C. Siegel, RH, is the country's foremost peak performance hypnotherapist. A nationally prominent author of 20+books, including Building Super Confidence, Winning At Life, Success Mind-Sets, and Living Invincibly Positive, for 26 years now he's personally worked with high-profile professional athletes and powerhouses in business and entertainment. You can review his acclaimed personal development programs at www.incrediblechange.com.]

Have you ever thought something through you said you *didn't* know how to deal with, and come up with an answer—the exact right answer—that surprised even yourself? Have you ever faced either an extreme adversity or crisis situation—one where you *had* to put your mind wholly into it—and you then made the specific *right* choices and decisions that served to move you through—and efficiently *beyond*—the situation?

Have you ever had a decisive need, or faced a notable challenge, or were caught up in a dilemma where all those friends outside you whom you asked for advice were either "too busy," "too disinterested," or gave you "dud" suggestions—and so you said "Ahhh the hell with it; I'll do the best *I* can by *myself*"—and then you *did?!*

Without ever meeting or knowing you, I can tell you the answers to all the preceding are a resounding *yes!* "Uh, why do you ask, Pete?" Why? Because I want you to understand that you are more capable, competent, creative, and mentally astute than you realize. Indeed, *a lot* more.

From 26 years as the country's foremost peak performance hypnotherapist, I've helped scores of people find—and connect with—inner resources and capacities they never even knew they possessed. And these empowering resources always moved them to realize one significant thing: They could look to *themselves* to find answers and direction that, heretofore, they believed they had to look outside themselves to find.

Once you realize this capacity, and trust its service potential within you, you can then *stop* hoping, waiting, wishing, dreaming, and depending on the "world" to bring you sustenance and assist your advance. You, literally, can go *within* and gain targeted understanding and insight that (essentially *always)* will be the exact right answer you need—the answer that, once applied, enables you to fulfill a need, sustain a quest, and/or expand your impact so you produce *further* progress and development.

WISDOM WITHIN, POWER WITHIN: YOUR SUBCONSCIOUS IS, IRREFUTABLY, A REALM OF PROVISION

"Are you telling me I don't have to ask those outside me for *any* advice or counsel?" No. I know that, many times, you must ask for others' opinions and perspectives. That—to a notable degree—is how you grow.

What I'm saying is that you can learn to trust and resourcefully use faculties, which you possess right now, to meet your individual needs, so you (of your *own* volition) can continue your advance. You are smarter than you realize; you are a lot more subconsciously capable than you even know:

- Your capacity for understanding is greater than you realize.
- Your capacity to attract the exact people you need into your life is greater than you realize.
- Your capacity for decisiveness is greater than you realize.
- Your capacity for thinking things through, thoroughly evaluating them, and letting your subcon-

scious provide you targeted insight and direction is greater than you realize.

- Your capacity to rise to the occasion, meet and master a demand, and glean the perspective necessary to devise and implement a plan of action—a plan for *success*—is greater than you realize.

After working with me, so many times clients, for decades now, have told me "Wow. I didn't know that I knew what I knew!" And my response to them is always the same. I tell them, "Interesting, huh? I wonder what *else* exists within your mental realm you're not aware of yet!" (The answer is, *a lot!*)

What does all this have to do with a mastermind group? Good question. Let me explain it like this: There are two general types of mastermind groups. The first is where you assemble a defined group of people who, presumably, bring to the table a variety of established knowledge and a desire to serve and, therefore, *be* served. This is the traditional mastermind structural framework.

If you establish one that works, where your members are consistent in their motivation and their enthusiasm to help you, great. My personal experience has been that, because of my high-profile reputation as a therapist and life transformation facilitator, I usually have my brain picked continually by eager-beaver mastermind group members who *want* something from me (for *their* personal lives), much more than wanting to truly help me out with a marketing and/or promotional situation I'm facing.

As far as I'm concerned, the rule of thumb with mastermind groups is this: Make sure the scales balance. There must be a decided balance between members genuinely giving *to* you and their personal expecting and requesting *of* you. If not, you're just essentially pouring water to help someone *else's* tree grow, while *your* tree doesn't receive the degree of nourishment *it* needs to grow, indeed, to ultimately flourish.

Which leads us nicely to the second kind of mastermind group: the Inner Counsel Think Tank. Remember the three initial questions I asked you, those where I said I knew your answers were a definitive yes?

Well, in *this* type of mastermind group, you'll now use your vast, untapped subconscious capacity to meet your personal needs. And, as such, you'll come to rely on your *own* mental power to get your life emphatically *done.*

Again, I'm not saying don't look to, seek out, or request the perceptions of others. I'm saying you can, and should, learn how to recognize your *own* life-sustaining/expanding power. And trust—and *apply* —this power so an "inner mastermind group" is working full time to enhance and increase your personal welfare.

YOUR INNER COUNSEL THINK TANK: USING YOUR OWN WISDOM, ABILITY, AND CREATIVITY TO SUPPLY THE ANSWERS YOU NEED

This process, as I personally teach it, is easy to implement and produces incredible results. Let me detail it for you now.

The Inner Counsel Think Tank Process

1. First, write down one specific thing that you feel you need direction and/or an answer for. This sets the stage for what your Inner Counsel will be meeting about.
2. For example: Are you looking for a title for your new book? Which person should you hire for an important position from your pool of candidates? What's the best way to approach asking your boss for a raise? How can you get on the radio or TV show you know you're qualified for—and that would really give your product or service the visibility lift you need?

Write this one focal point question down. And then, when you do, just consciously review it. And make notes regarding any ideas that may pop up. Then, say to yourself (and mean it), "Now, I'll turn this question over to my Inner Counsel. Their collective wisdom and insight knows *exactly* what to do and *how* to do it."

3.   Now you'll gain subconscious access, so first, seclude yourself in a quite, nondistracting environment, one where you're sure you'll not be disturbed. Take your phone off the hook, loosen any tight or binding clothing you may be wearing, and then position yourself on your back, lying either on your bed, the couch, or the floor or stretched out in a reclining chair so you feel totally comfortable and at ease.

Next, let your eyelids gently close and take three *l-o-n-g, d-e-e-p* breaths, inhaling easily through your nostrils and slowly exhaling through your mouth.

Next, envision yourself slowly descending a staircase of seven steps. And with each step, mentally/silently repeat the word *"D-O-W-N"* to yourself, allowing yourself to progressively let loose and more thoroughly mentally/physically relax with each successive step you descend.

When you've easily, comfortably reached the bottom step and are feeling the deep and soothing comfort of mind/body inner calmness, then shift your awareness so you perform the scope of the next three steps.

4.   Now you'll engage your Inner Counsel Think Tank. And so, imaginatively seated at a round table, clearly notice that there are four other members of your group seated at the table along with you:

- Creativity/new idea generator
- Wisdom/insight
- Motivation/will to triumph
- Marketing/promotion

You can imagine them as actual people or individual composites of condensed white light energy.

Take some time to imaginatively acknowledge them and say a heartfelt hello to each of the four members at the table with you.

5. Next, call the meeting to order. Looking at the group with a CEO's confident directness, tell them why you've convened them (e.g., "We're here today to discuss and give targeted insight to broaching the following issue").

Then, clearly tell them the question you've written down. Next, mentally go from person to person and ask them, for example, "Creativity/new idea generator—as *you* consider this, what have *you* to say?" Then, just comfortably wait for them to respond. They may readily give you some startling revelation. Or, they may say, "Hmmm ... let me think on it some more, and I'll be getting back to you shortly."

Whatever their response, tell them "Thank you." And then move on to engaging the *next* counsel member in the same outlined way.

After you've engaged each of the four members individually (and have acknowledged their response), inhale deeply and exhale through your mouth slowly.

Then, imaginatively sit back in your round table chair and look at them as a collective group and notice them speaking to and interacting with each *other* about your particular question.

Next, ask if they've come up with anything else. And let them answer you. Some more targeted revelation may be expressed, or they may say, "We'll *keep* working on it, and we'll be getting back to you very soon with *more* important, useful information and direction."

6. Finish your meeting with a genuine "Thank you *all!*" Then, with strong feeling, silently repeat the following affirmation: "This group gives me valuable insight each time we convene. They all have my best interest in mind. And they all know what to do, and *exactly* how to do it. I am now completely open to *continue* receiving their insight and direction!"

7. Again inhale a long deep breath through your nostrils and slowly exhale through your mouth. And now you're ready to return back to your full conscious awareness once again. So imagine you're now ascending a staircase of four steps, suggesting to yourself with each step you ascend that you are more alert and more completely consciously aware. Then, when you've reached the top step, let your eyelids open, inhale deeply, fill up your lungs, and *s-t-r-e-t-c-h.*

8. Now, take a pen and paper and write down *all* the information the counsel members provided you. Take your time here, and just let their

suggestions and direction easily stream through you and out onto your notepad.

9. When you've written down all related information your counsel members have provided you, proceed to organize it in an implementation hierarchy.

And then, one by one, start doing, applying, and/or tasking in accord with what they said.

THE STREAM OF INSIGHT WILL CONTINUE TO FLOW

As well as the information you wrote down from your postmeeting wrap-up, the group will likely continue supplying targeted information to you regarding handling and appropriately dealing with the question you posed.

Ideas and insight are sure to start popping up out of the blue—sometimes in the most unlikely places (e.g., while you're driving, grocery shopping, showering, working out, eating, on the phone, in the bathroom, reading, playing golf).

This is why I suggest you carry a pen and pad with you once you begin using this process. And, when you can (i.e., *not* while driving), write down the new insight your group has unfolded to you.

A FINAL REVIEW AND COMMENTARY

Always be sure to bring an air of patience and good willed expectancy to your Inner Counsel Think

Tank meetings. Don't force your members to comply, or put "*C'mon,* what's the answer here!" pressure on them. Just approach your contact with them as I've outlined to ensure maximum results.

I suggest you have Inner Counsel meetings no more than twice per week, with at least three days between each session. This is so your subconscious can process your request without being pressured and/or emotionally overloaded.

Once you've received what you know is the right, workable answer (and have implemented it successfully), you can then reconvene your group to address *another* need or question you may have.

Just use the exact format I've outlined each time. And know that the more you use this process, the more powerful, fruitful, and definitively substantive it will be for you!

17

COLLECTIVE GENIUS GROUPS How to Unlock the $100,000+Genius in You!

David Garfinkel

Each group member, thinking in perfect harmony with the others, creates a "Collective Genius," which allows an extraordinary increase in personal power and access to knowledge, skills, and experiences through a process that is proven time after time, but is mysterious, even today.

The Collective Genius is a nonphysical entity of thought that grows in strength and usefulness to each member of the group through the sustained effort and goodwill of each member. What was difficult or impossible yesterday becomes possible today and virtually guaranteed to come to completion in the surprisingly near future, when the principles of the Collective Genius are faithfully applied.

THE COLLECTIVE GENIUS

Note: The following is based on what author Napoleon Hill said in Chapter 6 of his book, *Master Key to Riches.*

Definition: The Collective Genius is "an alliance of two or more minds, blended in the spirit of perfect harmony and cooperating for the attainment of a definite purpose."

This is important, because in this definition you can find deep meaning that describes what is necessary to attain personal power—and *all* success is based, in part, on that. The Collective Genius principle is actually at the foundation of all human progress, whether on an individual or group level.

The most important word in the definition is *harmony.* Pay attention to that. For without harmony, collective effort may constitute cooperation, but it will fall short of having the power that harmony provides. And without that power, great achievement is not possible.

Here are some of the major benefits of Collective Genius:

Benefit 1: Through a Collective Genius group, you may receive the full benefit of the *experience, training, education, specialized knowledge,* and *native ability* of others—just as completely as if their minds were your own!

Benefit 2: When two or more minds are aligned in a spirit of *perfect* harmony for the attainment of a definite purpose, they stimulate each other with a high degree of inspiration—and that may become the state of mind known as Faith! (To get a slight idea of how powerful this stimulation is, think of what it's like to be with a close friend, or better yet, think of what it's like to be in love.)

Benefit 3: When the Collective Genius principle is actively applied, it has the effect of connecting you with the subconscious section of your mind—*and* the subconscious sections of your allies' minds. That means, in effect, you have full access to knowledge you never learned! This fact explains many of the seemingly miraculous results obtained through Collective Genius groups.

WHAT TO DO DURING A COLLECTIVE GENIUS GROUP MEETING

There are three roles members need to play:
1.   Leader
2.   Timekeeper
3.   Scribe

The role of the *leader* is to introduce the meeting, keep each member on the subject, moderate any disagreements, summarize what each member said during the meeting in a brief closing statement at the end of the meeting, and set the time for the next meeting.

The *timekeeper* lets members know when they have a few minutes left and when their time is up.

The role of the *scribe* is to take very concise and strategic minutes. Then, the scribe will send out in his or her minutes one week hence:

Date of Meeting:

Member 1: One-sentence summary of what's been going on for this person.

One-sentence summary of the goal or problem announced.

One-sentence summary of the goal to be accomplished by the next meeting.

These minutes should end with an announcement of when the next meeting will take place.

Note: These minutes are to be sent out ONE WEEK after the meeting, NOT right away. The reason for this is to serve as a reminder of what was promised and when the next meeting is at the midpoint between the two meetings. This will ensure maximum continuity of the group, as members may be too busy to communicate on the phone between meetings.

Regular meetings go like this:

2 minutes: Leader opens, welcomes, gets group started.

14 minutes: First group member speaks.

14 minutes: Second group member speaks.

14 minutes: Third group member speaks.

14 minutes: Fourth group member speaks.

2 minutes: Leader summarizes what each member said, sets meeting date for next meeting, asks if anyone needs "accountability"—a call from another member in a week to make sure you're on track—and closes meeting.

In meetings, each person's time should be used as follows:

First 5 minutes: Talk about what you've been doing.

Second 4 minutes: Talk about a goal or a problem.

Third 5 minutes: Group brainstorms solutions, and at end of time, you declare your finalized goal.

THE BEST ATTITUDE AND APPROACH

The best thing we can do is treat each member's goals and problems as if they are about a business that we personally have a financial and emotional stake in. That is, use our best managerial, coaching, and otherwise motivational skills to help the person speaking stay on track and accomplish most effectively and most productively.

I have noticed in my own consultations that the most ready response I have to offer can often err on the side of too enthusiastic or too critical. It's important that we offer enthusiastic support and constructive criticism to each other. I think it is of paramount importance that our comments, suggestions, observations, and questions be framed in such a way as not only to get the information across, but also to reach the person we're talking to in a way calculated to get the maximum instant understanding and the maximum acceptance.

In the pressure to deliver ideas quickly, there may be some slippage into cutting to the quick too quickly or boosting too generously. This is to be expected; after all, we're brainstorming. My point here is only that we should aim for this golden mean that does the very best job we can do to keep each other on track.

Here are some suggestions to implement this attitude and approach:

- *Use your most consultative focus.* Do what you can to let the member come to his or her own, right conclusion.
- *Keep it concise.* We would all like to have more information than time will reasonably allow. Go for only the key facts with your questions. In the real world you often have to make decisions based on insufficient information. That may be the case here from time to time.
- *Have fun.* Herb Cohen, the great negotiation teacher, talks about the difference between "idea opponents" and "personal opponents." Let's all do what we can to focus on behaviors and ideas, not issues of motivation and character! Let's make it fun to take our time as well as to offer advice.
- *Make it a priority.* The collective value of this hour we spend together is well over $1,000. You could make a case for its being worth upward of $10,000, if you add the highest paying use of each member. Treat the time the same way you would treat an asset valued between $1,000 and $10,000.

- *Focus on the member's agenda—not yours.* If someone wants to work on a problem or a goal that you think is the wrong problem or the wrong goal, the best service you can provide is to allow that person to discover it, sooner or later.

   Otherwise, he or she will never get the experience not to make the mistake again. Take members at their word that they want to be supported at what they say they want to be supported on. Help people with what they ask for help on.

- *This is about accomplishment—not activity.* It's not about best efforts and heroic intentions—it's about getting things done. Support yourself and the others in THAT.

18

THE SIMPLEST, FASTEST MASTERMIND GROUP

Phil Alexander*

[* Phil Alexander is currently putting the finishing touches on his guru course: How to Be the Dominant Guru in Your Niche. Check out his many guru resources at http://www.philalex.com.]

My phone rang. I glanced at the clock. 11:03P.M.? It's either a wrong number, an emergency, or an insomniac telemarketer.

It was none of the above. Well, not really. It was an emergency of sorts. My pal was speaking at a seminar and needed a "Wow" exhibit to fill a hole in his presentation. Did I have one? Sure. Could I brainstorm on how to best present it at the seminar and enhance his guru status? Of course. Could I e-mail them as attachments as soon as possible? Not a problem. This fellow is one of my oldest and dearest friends in the information marketing business, and I'd love to help, as he's helped me more than once.

Calls like this come in frequently if you are plugged into an active network. Small networks, big networks, they all work, and usually, work great.

Most people think that bigger is better when it comes to mastermind groups. I don't think so. Bigger isn't better or worse, but it's certainly different.

Small groups are the most efficient and productive way to mastermind, in my experience.

And why is the group size so important, you ask?

The number of people in the group is one of the critical factors in a mastermind. Every single person you add to the mix is another source of ideas and another wall to bounce ideas off of.

Each person added has a reaction to and chemistry and relationship with everyone else. Add more people, and you can't help but cause friction.

In mathematical terms, you are exponentially increasing the chances of conflict, but only linearly increasing the areas of expertise.

Most long-term mastermind groups have between 6 and 20 people. If you can keep 25 people working in harmony without the present threat of physical violence, you're a better man than I am, Gunga Din.

So, let's talk about your first mastermind group. Let's keep it small.

What's the smallest number of people you need to make a mastermind group?

One? Well, one really isn't a mastermind group.

It's two. Can two people talking be considered a mastermind? Isn't talking between two people normally just called "conversation"?

You may not have thought of a two-person conversation as a mastermind group. But if your conversation partner offers any or all of the benefits of a mastermind group—and has a phone—you're in business.

Some conversations have changed my mind, my outlook, and on certain occasions, my life.

Two people can form a potent mini-mastermind group—and of the most powerful, because the two of you can focus on the smallest topic, zero in on exactly what needs to be discussed, and—if necessary—turn on a dime.

ADVANTAGES

Make no mistake—there are a lot of benefits to a small mastermind group. Here are a few.

Ease

Scheduling a mastermind group with a large number of people is an exercise in diplomacy that would make the UN sit up and take notice. However, a two-person mastermind, obviously, is the fastest to arrange and implement. And as we all know, what's easy to implement has the best chance of getting done.

You just can't beat the ease and convenience of picking up the phone and calling someone. If you need a quick and easy answer, a two-person mastermind can get the job done faster than just about anything else. Masterminding purists will insist that face-to-face masterminding is best. They are right. But with travel the way it is now, going to Zaire for a 15-minute chat isn't a rational use of time.

Focus

Like it or not, every large mastermind group will have some difference of opinion. It's this difference that makes it so valuable! But sometimes, a small two or three-person group can bust out from a larger group to talk about something specific. It keeps the larger mastermind on track, retains focus, and respects the larger group's time. Masterminds can wither away if members find the focus shifting from what they originally joined up for. These small bust-out or breakout masterminds keep the larger group on track.

Privacy

In the "fantasy entrepreneur" world, everything gets shared, no one poaches or discloses confidential information, and everyone is rational, all the time. Well, in the real world, like it or not, you can't disclose the whole deal, because some people aren't in sync with every part. Admittedly, free sharing of information is one of the hallmarks of a good mastermind group. But some information is so sensitive, embarrassing, or dangerous it can't be disclosed with the membership at large. Furthermore, some people are so opposed to a certain viewpoint that a small bust-out group can, and should, be formed.

Equality

One member can't dominate the group. Well, he can, but he may end up talking to a dial tone. Unless you're a glutton for punishment, you won't mastermind with someone who takes and takes, and then takes some more.

That sort of domination is sometimes more likely in a larger group. But it's important to be clear on the difference between domination and someone just expressing a conflicting viewpoint, which isn't a problem—unless he or she is doing it to be disruptive.

DISADVANTAGES

Okay, so what's the problem with these small groups?

Idea Limitations

Like it or not, if your mastermind group is just you and 1 other person, you'll reach the hard limit of ideas a lot quicker than if there are 20 people in the room. You can manage this by picking well-informed mastermind partners in the first place, but ultimately, when your partner in a two-person mastermind runs dry of ideas, you have to hang up and call someone else.

Idea Sparks

When you throw a bunch of different people in a room to solve a problem, idea creation starts to feed on itself. One person will come up with a germ of an idea, then a second will add something to it, a third will get rid of a potential problem, and a fourth will add the finishing touch. Of course, sometimes a fifth will take all the credit, but that's part of the risk you run.

TIPS FOR MAXIMIZING YOUR TWO-PERSON MASTERMIND

These six tips are critical to running any mastermind group that meets by phone, especially a two-member group.

No Interruptions

I'm astonished at the number of people who sweat blood to get an important and busy person on the phone for a mastermind call.

When you are scheduling a mastermind, be mindful of distractions that could sap the attention of the participants. When arranging larger mastermind groups, it's not uncommon to have an unwritten rule to have cell phones set to vibrate and laptops with their e-mail alerts turned off.

It's easy to get sloppy when a mastermind consists of only you and another person. Too easy to flip open that telephone, hit speed dial, and talk. Instant gratification.

Real mastermind calls are too valuable for spur-of-the-moment conversations. I keep a text file on my desktop that has a list of people I regularly talk to. Every time I think of something to say next time we talk, a little memo goes by their name. When we talk or I send off an e-mail, I have a list of things to talk about. It keeps things moving and keeps my interruption of their time to a minimum.

Wasting time is the cancer of the informal two-person call. Don't waste time with trivia, and have a deadline. Being behind the 8 ball with regard to a deadline is a fantastic way to keep on track. If you don't think so, go into a 20-minute master-mind with only 15 minutes of time!

No Call Waiting

It's a comedic staple: You're on the phone with someone, it's an important call, and the other person's call waiting goes off.

Does he see who it is? Does he chat with the caller and bump you to second-class status? Almost as bad: He doesn't answer it, and the call-waiting beep interrupts every other phrase! My take: It's completely inappropriate. Most mastermind calls should be short, scheduled, and to the point. Call waiting becomes irrelevant in that case.

Preplanning

I met a fellow once who was the number 1 salesperson in his company every single year. Every year, they would try to get him to teach his secrets to the other salespeople.

Get this: He was willing to teach his method, but the other salespeople weren't interested in learning. Another thing: He had only one secret. One. And he freely disclosed it.

What was it?

Preplanning the appointment.

Seriously, that was his secret. Planning. This guy was a *bear* for planning. He would plan everything. He even set a time limit for the meeting.

Kind of busts the "natural salesperson" myth, I know. Deep down, many people believe that the best salespeople are like brilliant improvisational comics, the Robin Williams of selling, able to pull the magical closing sentence out of the air to win the deal. In reality, most of what appear to be off-the-cuff improvs are nothing of the sort—they're tightly scripted routines that the comedian or salesperson memorizes in advance to pull out at just the right moment.

In his words: "I'm a traveling salesman, basically. My time is money. Sure, the travel part of the business is a big part of what I do, but some customers, because of their volume and profit potential, are only worth a certain amount of money, and therefore, only a certain amount of time. If the time requirement is too large and the profit too small, I either try to service them on the phone or cut 'em loose."

"Oh, and by preplanning the appointment, I also preplan common objections and responses to them. In fact, I try to negate the common objections in the sales presentation ... up front."

Wise words indeed.

Plans are of little importance, but planning is everything.

—Winston Churchill

Planning a telephone call is far more than coloring in a few blocks on a wall calendar. The most successful entrepreneurs plan everything to the maximum degree that they can. They know that you can't plan for the unknown. When the unknown rises up and rears its ugly head, it's a good thing that part of the deal is planned!

And of course, sometimes the unknown that appears is so incredible that all the planning you did previously is wasted. This is often used as an excuse by the lazy not to plan. Not true. Having a plan in place is tremendously refreshing.

Have an Agenda

If you have an agenda, or schedule, send it to your mastermind partner a few days ahead of time.

These little bullet points of things you want to cover will reside in your partner's subconscious, and you'll have a better prepared mastermind, even if he or she doesn't think about it!

If you've spent any time at all in corporate America, you've been to a meeting with an agenda. Your e-mail or in-box will have a list of things you are going to discuss, distributed well in advance of the meeting. A time limit for the meeting and an agenda, together, push you to make the best use of your time. There aren't many things the seat-of-the-pants entrepreneur can take from big corporations. Having an agenda in front of a meeting is one of them.

Make the Call

And while we're on the subject of telephone calling, who calls who? Please, don't be a cheapskate and insist your partner call you so you won't have to pay for the long distance. It's far, far better, even with a scheduled phone call, that you make it, because then you are the one in control.

Take Notes or Record the Conversation

You just can't keep it all in your head. At least, I can't. Little things get said that are quickly forgotten. A recording, written notes, or something similar can be the memory jog to stir up that contact, idea, or connection weeks, months, or even years later.

I've actually done a fair bit of study on organizing information, because my desk is constantly awash with paper. What I've found is this: The best organizers use a variety of ways to keep track of their information, schedule, and planning. But everything, and I mean everything, gets crammed into one device or product. In other words, they may take notes on a napkin at lunch, write an idea on a lunch receipt, and make a note to call a client on a matchbook, but that night, when the pockets get emptied, it all gets transferred into their main device.

Personally, I use my iBook to schedule, plan, and keep track of stuff. But when I'm away from home, I stick with a small paper pad, called the Claire Fontaine Rhodia. It's 3 inches by 4 inches. Cheap, and functions as a de facto scratch pad, planner, and note taker.

DO YOU REALLY NEED A TWO-PERSON MASTERMIND CALL?

When you think about it, masterminding is all about finding solutions to problems. But sometimes you don't need a solution. Sometimes, all you need is an *answer.*

I've become a real information resource for many entrepreneurs I've met, and it's not uncommon for a fax to groan in over the machine as I'm working late at night, asking for some rare book or information product. I appreciate these people faxing or e-mailing me because a message on my answering machine, or a direct call, is much more inconvenient, and an interruption as well.

What's the difference between a solution and an answer? An answer is usually more absolute. Faster to produce.

Point being: Don't waste time on masterminding when an answer will do.

Asking for an answer is not the same as a mastermind. The exchange of information in an answer call is one-way. A mastermind is two-way. An answer is an imposition; a mastermind is, and must be, a cooperation. If you need an answer, a quick one, don't intrude on the person's personal time—most gurus' schedules are far too structured to permit interruptions anyway!

At this point you might be asking: Doesn't this sound kind of strident and narrow-minded? Don't any of your planned mastermind calls go overtime? Don't you ever talk about anything that isn't work?

I'm sure what I'm saying makes me sound like a workaholic Mr. Spock. Sure, sometimes my mastermind calls can wander into topics of mutual interest. But that's the key: mutual. We all have memories of being bored to tears on long calls where the subject being discussed had no relevance or interest to us.

19

HOW A MASTERMIND GROUP CAN TRANSFORM YOUR CAREER

Mitch Meyerson*

[* 163 Mitch Meyerson is the author of four books, including Success Secrets of the Online Marketing Superstars and Six Keys to Creating the Life You Desire. He also has co created The Guerrilla Marketing Coaching Program, Product Factory, and Traffic School. For more information, visit www.MitchMeyerson.com.]

The idea of a mastermind group is certainly not new, but given today's ever changing and competitive business environment, it has never been more relevant. With the online and offline landscapes changing at an unprecedented pace, the small to midsize business owner must assess these changes and adapt quickly. And more than ever, we need to partner with peers and colleagues in a way that generates fresh ideas, leverages databases, and ensures accountability.

Over the past few years I have been a part of a mastermind group that has literally changed the focus of my online business. This mastermind group consists of five successful coaches who bring enthusiasm, creativity, and openness to our weekly discussions.

One of the most important topics brought up in this group was the changing landscape of the coaching industry. With the enormous growth of the Internet and the rapidly increasing number of coaches in the marketplace, the competition was getting very steep, information was ever present, and the redundancy of offerings by coaches was apparent. We had discussions on trends in the industry and speculated on the future of the profession.

Questions are critical in mastermind groups. Some of the ones we discussed were these: What are customers really looking for? What type of offering will be remarkable? What is the true need given current market conditions? The answers we came up with were community, product development, strong leaders, and accountability to a result in a relatively short time frame.

One point of agreement is the need for coaches to have their own information products to help position themselves as experts in their niche. Although there were a few ebooks on the subject, there was no online learning environment that actually helped entrepreneurs create their own products through a step-by-step system in a set period of time.

In a mastermind brainstorming session, one of the members, Michael Port, and I came up with the idea to create The Product Factory, an online learning and coaching community that would allow students to create their products in 90 days or less (www.90Day Product.com). This program used our mastermind research on building community, accessing Internet-based technology, and creating an intensive time-limited program. This ultimately became one of the most successful programs on the Internet and led to another groundbreaking program called Traffic School (www.TrafficSchoolSystem.com).

As you can see, mastermind groups are a great model for synergy and teamwork. Rather than approaching fellow business owners from a competitive standpoint based on win-lose interactions, mastermind groups approach relationships from a collaborative view that values free-flowing ideas and flexible boundaries. With this type of mind-set and the right group of people, everyone's a winner.

In summary, mastermind groups can help business owners in a multitude of ways:

- Brainstorming new products and services
- Creating community
- Expanding resources and increasing exposure
- Creating systems of accountability
- Getting support and encouragement
- Creating synergistic results where the whole equals much more than the sum of the parts

Today's digitally based world has brought tremendous technological advances and opportunities, but also has brought a certain level of detachment among people. In addition to creating the type of results described here, mastermind groups are a great way to fill an important need in today's society: bringing back the human connection.

20

EXPLOSIVE DANCES OF CREATIVITY

Bob Scheinfeld*

[* Bob Scheinfeld is the best-selling author of The Invisible Path to Success and The 11th Element. His passion is helping others carve out and live what he calls their "Ultimate Lifestyle." For more information, visit: http://www.bobscheinfeld.com.]

The world's most successful and admired people are often called "creative," and creativity is a highly sought after talent and skill. People who are naturally creative or find a way to tap into their creativity are able to solve problems, come up with new ideas and approaches to enhance the success or efficiency of projects, and push the envelope of what's possible in the world.

But how do you stimulate creativity, open to it, create an explosive dance of creativity when you want or need to? One way that I've found is the mastermind group.

Whenever I've been part of a mastermind group as a participant or the focal point of the group, I'm always amazed at the dynamic that gets created. People who aren't normally "idea people" suddenly start coming up with amazing ideas, and people who are ordinarily creative or idea people seem to take their skills to a higher level. It's an amazing phenomenon.

A big key, of course, is that the structure of a mastermind group has a core rule that participants must be free to share whatever they feel motivated to share—no judgments, no criticisms, no limits.

From my experience, there are two forms of learning:
1. Direct learning
2. Collision learning

Direct learning is when someone says "X" to you and you find "X" to be valuable. Collision learning is when someone says "X" to you and, whether "X" is valuable to you or not, it makes you think of "Y," and "Y" is extremely valuable to you.

The creative dance that comes from mastermind groups has direct and collision dynamics. Sometimes someone comes up with an idea, shares it, and other members of the group find it valuable. At other times, one person says one thing, another person says another thing, and those two ideas cause someone else to come up with a third "collision idea," which is considered even more valuable.

In my own case, when I'm participating in a mastermind group and feel motivated to share something in response to a question or problem that's on the table, I'm often amazed at what comes out of my mouth. "Where did that come from?" I ask myself.

A brilliant title for one of my best-selling books came from a participant in a mastermind group. I'd been struggling with what to call the book and was talking about the core concept of it when a lightbulb suddenly went off in the other person.

Because of the power of the creative dynamic in mastermind groups, my grandfather, Aaron Scheinfeld, founder of Manpower, Inc., the world's largest temporary help service and a Fortune 500 company, set up a conference center in the Midwest specifically to create opportunities for management teams to mastermind with each other while away from their familiar environments. He was a big believer in the power of the mastermind.

The older I get, the more time I want to spend in the state I call "creative ecstasy." It's one of the most enjoyable states I experience in life. Because of that, in recent years, I've shifted what I do and how I do it in my life and business activities to spend more and more time in that energy. Being in a mastermind group facilitates being in that kind of energy for long periods of time, and I love it.

21

THE BENEFITS OF A MASTERMIND

Dr. Larina Kase (www.PAScoaching.com)

The benefits of a mastermind group are conveyed in the name: Two or four or six or eight minds are certainly better than one. Together, you've created a mastermind that is extremely powerful.

As a psychologist, I know that we have limits on our mental capacity and can easily get stuck in mental ruts and mind traps. The members of your group help you see possibilities you never envisioned and give you a reality check when your seemingly great visions are not feasible.

We might think we've come up with a million-dollar idea, but we're just remembering something filed away in our minds—something that has been done before. This happened to me once, and I was fortunate enough to have colleagues who let me know that my wonderful original idea wasn't so original after all!

We sometimes get so married to our ideas that we evaluate their worth in a biased manner. Keep this in mind when forming your mastermind group—include people who aren't shy about pushing you to question your own assumptions and sell your idea to them.

They can serve as a mirror of the marketplace and can help you think of potential objections and difficulties before you spend too much time and energy and learn the lesson the hard way.

Another wonderful aspect of a mastermind group is the mental synergy that can be created. I was once in a group in which several of the members came upon the same revelation—and it wasn't even during the group, it was in the week in between. It's like a relay race: One person grabs the baton, runs with it, and passes it on. You could do it on your own, but your performance will be much faster, better, and more enjoyable with your team.

The other thing that I've loved about groups is the support and education. You get to celebrate, learn from, and get inspired by one another's successes and accomplishments. You can hold each other accountable for following through with activities and get new ideas and market research. If someone in your group tried out a particular strategy and gained information about what works and doesn't work, you can benefit from his or her research and experiences.

Realize that the group is powerful, and as much as it can help you, it can hurt you.

Remember that the people you surround yourself with will help you create your own reality. If your group consists of people who like to dwell on problems, complain, or commiserate with each other, the energy of the group will drain you rather than invigorate you.

To make your group and the mental synergy process most effective, select group members who are creative, open, positive, intuitive, supportive, expressive about their opinions, and devoted to achievement. Include people whom you genuinely believe in, respect, and want to succeed because these are the people you can best help and who can best help you.

22

THE SEVEN SECRETS OF SUCCESSFUL MASTERMINDING

Andy Fuehl*

[* Andy Fuehl is an international trainer on money and business psychology and is the author of the best sellers Wealth Without a Job: The Entrepreneur's Guide to Freedom and Security beyond the 9 to 5 Lifestyle and Profiting in Turbulent Times and the upcoming Revealed: Hidden Strategies of a Real Estate Tycoon: The Inner Thinking of Dolf de Roos. Andy went from being unemployed to a millionaire in under three years using the same techniques he now teaches. You can find Andy Fuehl on the Internet at AndyFuehl.com, WealthWithoutaJob.com, or StrategiesOfaTycoon.com.]

Why form a mastermind group? If you are serious about being hugely successful in business, you must form a mastermind group. I know you are serious, otherwise you wouldn't be reading this great book. I used the method of masterminding to go from being unemployed to being a millionaire in under three years. And so can you.

All great achievers over time were part of a mastermind group. People like Thomas Edison, Henry Ford, and Charles Schwab. Edison and Ford both had little education. However, both were extremely successful in business because they used a mastermind approach.

New and better ideas come from the mastermind, which Napoleon Hill refers to as the "Third Mind." The Third Mind is created when two or more minds come together focused on a common cause.

I have formed several mastermind teams. The teams range from 2 to 12 people and focus on different areas: investing, growing your business, marketing, and authoring books. Each group has a specific focus.

I will share with you the seven secrets to create and maintain a successful mastermind group:
1. You must have a team with a variety of viewpoints and backgrounds.
2. Pick a leader to guide the group.
3. Develop a common goal.
4. Have an agenda.
5. Keep an open mind.
6. Dedicate a set time and have regular meetings.
7. Have fun.

SECRET 1

People on your team must come from different industries or areas of expertise because you want different perspectives. When building on, combing, or rearranging ideas from different perspectives, a better idea is usually formed.

Some of the best ideas I have received were formulated using a mastermind team. I have published two books, *Wealth Without a Job* and *Profiting in Turbulent Times,* using the mastermind method. The powerful concepts came from using the Third Mind, which comes from the mastermind team.

SECRET 2

Pick a leader for teams of five or more. The leader guides and keeps the team on track and helps everyone stay open-minded during the idea-generating process. This is critical to the team's success.

SECRET 3

Develop a common goal. A team is effective only when the outcome or goal is clear. Most mastermind teams lack vision and a common objective and thus fail.

SECRET 4

Have an agenda. An agenda is critical and keeps the mastermind team focused during the meeting.

SECRET 5

Each member of the mastermind team must remain completely open. When ideas are first presented, just write them down without editing. After all the ideas have been expressed, examine each one. Build on each idea to come up with better ideas. Then pick the most effective idea and take action.

SECRET 6

Effective mastermind groups meet weekly, bimonthly, or monthly. Consistent, regular meetings are essential. At bare minimum, the group must meet once per month, otherwise momentum and enthusiasm decline.

SECRET 7

Have fun. This is the most important element. If you and everyone in your mastermind are having fun, the quality of the ideas will go up.

Remember the seven secrets to a successful mastermind team and go out and take action now. Action is required to achieve your goals. So go ahead and come up with some big goals and put your mastermind team into action.

To your success!

23

MULTIPLY YOUR IDEAS WITH YOUR MASTERMIND

Cathy Stucker*

[* As the Idea Lady, Cathy Stucker helps authors, professionals, and entrepreneurs attract customers and make themselves famous with creative strategies that make marketing easy, inexpensive, and even fun! Learn how Cathy can help you grow your business with publicity, online and offline marketing, and more at www.idealady.com. Be sure to sign up for her mailing list to get free marketing tips and resources.]

Because I am known as the Idea Lady, people often ask me for the secret to coming up with great ideas. It's simple: The more input your brain receives, the greater its out-put can be.

So what happens when you join with someone else, increasing the input to your brain by sharing information and working together to create ideas? You might think that together you would be twice as effective. In fact, there is a synergistic effect that causes the number and quality of the ideas you generate together to increase beyond simple addition. In this case, 1+1 equals much more than 2.

Now imagine what happens when you join with several others, all focused on helping each other to succeed. Imagine exponentially increasing your knowledge, experience, and creativity by a factor of 6, 8, 12, or more. What could you accomplish then?

The power of a mastermind group goes beyond the simple exchange of information and ideas. The synergy created by the group helps each member to become greater than he or she is alone.

Have you ever noticed that when you think about something, it comes to you? The energy you create attracts what you desire. With all of the members focusing on creating success for each other, the energy of the group can create success on a grand scale.

The exact form of your mastermind group, how often you meet, the agenda of your meetings, and other details, are important but the most important aspect of the mastermind is that you take action. Join or start a group, then actively participate. Here are some ways to maximize the effectiveness of your mastermind group:

- *Choose people with backgrounds and experiences that are different from yours.* The more varied the perspectives of the people you invite to join, the more you can contribute to each other. Look for people from different fields and educational backgrounds but who share a commitment to action.

- *Meet in a comfortable location, where you can easily converse.* Noisy restaurants where you must shout to be heard are not conducive to creativity.

If your group meets over the telephone, encourage everyone to find a pleasant place from which to call. Using a headset telephone can reduce the stress and discomfort that can come from holding a telephone for long periods.

- *Create an environment where ideas can flow freely.* Encourage members to share without judgment. Several research studies have indicated that listening to Mozart can improve your thinking and reasoning. Playing your favorite Mozart sonata in the background during the mastermind meeting couldn't hurt!

- *Choose a meeting time when members are most productive.* Some people are in top form in the morning, others don't hit their stride until the afternoon, and some do their best work late at night. If your group contains an assortment of morning people and night owls, meet at varying times to take advantage of everyone's prime time.

- *Know what you want from your mastermind and what you are willing and able to give.* You may want your mastermind group to provide advice and support in a particular area of your business. Remember that giving is at least as important as receiving. Look for opportunities to help the members of your mastermind reach their goals.

- *Select a meeting format that allows everyone to be involved.* Whether you focus on one member per meeting, or give each member equal time during the meeting, all members should have the chance to give and receive.

- *Have an effective way of capturing ideas.* Some groups designate one person to record the ideas generated during a session and distribute the list to everyone. You may find that having to write down what is being discovered slows the process. I like to record the session and make the recording available. (Of course, members must agree not to share the recordings with anyone outside the group.) Each person then has an unfiltered record of exactly what happened. As you listen to the recording of a meeting, you may find ideas that you missed the first time around. It may be that you were not ready to hear the idea the first time.

- *Encourage members to share their favorite brain food—things that teach them, motivate them, excite them, or enlighten them.* These might be books, music, movies, articles, quotations, organizations, web sites, software programs, classes, games, or anything that stimulates the mind.

Joining forces with others to work together for each other's success enables all of us to achieve more. Sharing your brain power means generating more ideas, and the support of your mastermind will help you to implement those ideas and reach your goals.

24

TURNING LIFE INTO A SUCCESS STORY How a Former U.S. Marine and College Dropout Turned His Life into a Success Story

Tom Beal[3] (www.TomBeal.com)

You are about to learn how to take your life from where it is today to living the life of your dreams by tapping into one of the easiest ways possible: the power of a mastermind alliance.

First, let us briefly discuss and analyze two quotes you may have seen before:

Quote 1: *Success is something you attract by the person you become. Work hard on your job and you'll earn a living. Work hard on yourself and you'll earn a fortune.*

---

[3] Tom Beal, a 33-year-old former U.S. marine and college dropout who now masterminds with numerous best-selling authors, millionaire marketers, and top professional athletes, tells you how you can do it, too.

—Jim Rohn (best-selling author and

motivational speaker)

No one of importance or significance will desire to mastermind, associate, or work with you if you cannot contribute significant value. No one of importance will take you on as a coaching client if you cannot contribute significant value in return (HUGE key to my success/contact base).

Become a successful person and successful people will beat a path to your door.

How can you become a successful person?

Choose to become a serious student of life!

1. Become a coaching client of someone who has accomplished what you desire to attain.
2. Read books related to your passions and goals.
3. Attend live teleseminars with experts.
4. Listen to prerecorded interviews and lessons online.
5. Tap into local chapters of Toastmasters and Business Network International.
6. Get a library card and check out some audio programs (tapes/CDs) on personal and business development. Listen and take notes!

Then implement the tips, techniques, and strategies learned!

Quote 2: *Your income will be the average of [the income of] your five closest friends.*

—Jim Rohn

That quote explains itself!

Let me ask you a simple question: Do you want more wealth?

Of course you do, or you wouldn't be reading this book!

Here's a simple answer: Get wealthier friends!

Why?

When you're dealing with people who are creating miracles or enormous results and you're witnessing them as they occur, not only do you begin believing in miracles and enormous results, but you also begin expecting and creating them yourself.

Your levels of belief in *what is possible* reach new heights.

It's the law of association! And the power of a mastermind!

Call it success by osmosis.

How?

The answer to getting wealthier friends could be in a book over 250 pages long, or I could answer it in three words: *Attend live seminars.*

My life has been absolutely transformed in all areas, especially financially, by choosing to attend live seminars.

Side note: You do not need money overflowing in the bank when you first decide to attend seminars. You just need to CHOOSE to be there! Your future depends on it!

As a matter of fact, many times I freeloaded with other people going to the same event, slept in my car, and basically did whatever it took to get there—sometimes without money for food or a hotel room.

One time I went to a very costly event that drained the last dollar I had in my bank account and pocket. From that event I landed a joint venture deal with a friend that has forever changed my life.

Because I took a big risk with no guarantees, and because I went to that event well prepared and full of extreme value (see Step 1), expecting miracles, one manifested.

How do you stand out from the crowd?

Copy a success strategy dating back to Napoleon Hill, then emulated by Tony Robbins, Dr. Joe Vitale, and even me.

See if you can guess what that strategy is by taking a look at one of my newest web sites: http://www.mlm-experts.com.

You tell me what you think that strategy is and, more important, how you can begin applying it to your life and success immediately!

Make Today Great and God Bless!

25

IT'S TIME FOR PLAN B—BRAINSTORMING Playing the Brain Game for Gain

Craig Harrison*

[* Based in the San Francisco Bay Area, professional speaker Craig Harrison founded Expressions of Excellence!™ to provide sales and service solutions through speaking. For information on keynotes, training, coaching, curriculum for licensing, and more, visit www.ExpressionsOfExcellence.com or call (888)450-0664. E-mail excellence@craigspeaks.com for inquiries.]

Our work group was in the middle of a spirited brainstorming session—a free-form session where creativity is encouraged, judgment is suspended, and the best ideas often come after 10 or more minutes. The ideas were flying fast and furious, as they should when the group gets momentum. The energy was intoxicating. And, in a fit of inspiration, one employee suggested, "Why don't we reverse the order of the deliverables?"

While nine other people energetically accepted this offer as worthy of inclusion on their flip chart of ideas, their manager scowled, "That will never work!"

Thus ended a productive brainstorming session. Sadly, the manager was unclear on the concept at play. She replaced a brainstorm with a brain fart and stunk up the entire process.

A DIFFERENT KIND OF COLLABORATION

Brainstorming is a special type of meeting, with its own ground rules, tempo, and ethos. It's also an invaluable tool for idea generation, problem solving, innovation, team building, and creativity. Whether you are tasked with creating new sales contests or new strategic initiatives or simply trying to break out of the doldrums of your day-to-day routine, brainstorming carries the day.

RULES THAT ROCK!

By definition, brainstorming is unlike typical meetings. It's unbounded by traditional rules where designated people speak on predetermined subjects for prescribed times. Like a jam session of jazz musicians, all you need to do is begin recording and let the sounds begin. Remember, the key is to record it all. Later you can go back and edit out what might not be considered beautiful music.

In brainstorming sessions everyone is equal, all ideas are worthy of consideration, all judgment is suspended, and a person's rank or status is irrelevant. The goal is to fill the air with ideas, depart from conventional thinking, and allow the smorgasbord of strategies, ideas, inspirations, and epiphanies to cross-pollinate each other. Think of brainstorming meetings as magnificent melting pots, a veritable giant stew bowl where bouillabaisse bubbles and bursts, unleashing new, exciting, and innovative initiatives. Consider a skilled facilitator for best results, though this isn't a requirement.

THE B-LIST: PREPARING FOR YOUR MEETING

The following recommendations will ensure a successful session, whether it's a stand-alone brainstorm or part of a larger meeting or event:

- Adorn your environment with art, toys, games, crayons, colored markers, or other stimuli to get the juices flowing and invite fun, free thinking, and playfulness.
- Send special written invitations to set the tone, expectations, and goals for the session.
- Create a mental and/or physical ice breaker to loosen everyone up.
- Consider lava lamps, beanbag chairs, and even bubblegum and bubble makers to loosen everyone up.

- Encourage participation by all.
- Language is key. Use sentences such as "What if we...?," "How about...?," "Let's try...," or "Suppose we...?"
- Check your skepticism, negativity, and ego at the door. It's not about whose ideas are embraced. All should be, for the benefit of the group.
- Employ the "Yes, AND..." approach instead of a "Yes, BUT..." stance in response to others' ideas.
- Remind people to suspend judgment throughout the session.
- Assign a scribe or tape-record the meeting.
- Allow enough time for people to loosen up. Often the best ideas occur once the group has gotten over any self-consciousness and gathered momentum.
- Have fun!

Remember, like mastermind groups, brainstorming sessions rely on the reality that when multiple brain-power is applied, the results are greater than the sum of their parts. You will generate great results from the blend of talent, experience, ideas, and perspectives that naturally result from giving everyone equal footing and freeing them of the usual restrictions of time, structure, and rules.

By the way, what if...?

26

MASTERMINDING FOR MUSICIANS

Bill Hibbler

As you know from the introduction, I was in the music industry for over 20 years, and my first mastermind group was a music biz group.

If you're in a band, in a way, you're in a mastermind, but I want you to look at this differently. And although there's nothing wrong with having members of your band in your mastermind, I recommend forming one with people outside the band.

For one thing, you'll be able to speak freely if you're having problems in the band. For another, you'll benefit more by having outside people. After all, you've already got access to your band members and can mastermind with them in regular band meetings. Plus, you probably already spend a lot of time with the people in your band. It's good to have some time away from them.

If you're in a band, the ideal people to form a mastermind group with are band leaders from groups musically similar to yours. It's not essential, but being in the same or similar genre opens up a lot of opportunities for gigs and other promotions that won't work if you've got a mastermind group where one person does country, another does jazz, another blues, another rock, and you're a rapper.

Also, the reason I suggest working with other band leaders is that they'll be free to make decisions on behalf of their group. Or at least they will be a strong influence. That becomes important if you decide to do a show together or go in on a piece of gear or rehearsal space or any number of other projects you might consider.

Same thing goes if you're a solo artist or a songwriter. If possible, work with people in your genre.

In addition to the brainstorming benefits we've talked about throughout this book, a music industry group can open up a lot of doors for you.

For one thing, you can pool resources. You can negotiate better deals with rehearsal halls, music stores, and recording studios. In the case of the rehearsal hall, you can also share with some or all of the other members.

You can organize shows together. If you've tried to book your band, you know how hard it can be to get into certain rooms. If you usually get only 20 or 30 regulars at your show, that's not going to impress a lot of club owners.

On the other hand, if you've got four, five, or even six bands with similar-size followings, you can promote the groups as a package and guarantee a much larger audience.

Of course, club owners may point out that they book five or six bands a night all the time and some groups draw and others don't. If that comes up, you can point out that your situation is different. If they do it the usual way, some bands will put up flyers, some will call everyone they know, but others will do nothing, resulting in a mediocre night.

Here's why things will be different if they book you. And by the way, you can set up a temporary mastermind with several groups or artists for the sole purpose of promoting an event like this.

Rather than the usual cheap flyers, if you pool your money, you can afford to have a nice poster done. And rather than having just four or five people putting them up, you'll be able to mobilize 20 to 30 band members, plus friends, family, roadies, and so on.

You'll also be able to send out a sharp-looking postcard advertising the show to the combined mailing list of all the groups. You could also consider purchasing 30-second spots on latenight radio. Usually those spots are cheap, sometimes $5 or $10 each, because the only people listening at that hour are night owls and hardcore music fans. That may not excite the station's usual advertisers, but those are the exact people you're trying to reach. Radio ads would normally be out of reach for a single group, but by pooling your money, you can afford them.

With a little creativity and the power of the mastermind, rather than another night at the club, your gig becomes an *event* with a buzz.

My friend Roger Igo managed and played in a funk band in Houston. He worked together with a couple of other local funk bands to put on a series of shows, which they called The Texas Funk Syndicate. Kind of a local version of Lollapalooza or Lilith Fair.

You could do the same thing. You're far more likely to get noticed by the local media that way, too. It's about building a buzz.

The fun doesn't stop there, either. You can make your show more professional, more organized, and more entertaining using the power of the mastermind.

How, you ask? Good question.

First of all, do you have to rent a trailer, van, or truck when you do a gig? Instead, have everyone go in on one truck. Or there might be someone in your mastermind group that has one. Even if every band has its own van, you can save gas money by using fewer vehicles and hauling each other's gear.

For that matter, you can also share gear. That may not be comfortable for some drummers, but chances are you can share some of the backline. Not only will you have less gear to carry, but it'll make set changes go much faster.

Do you have a road crew for your band? Maybe you have one person who helps out. By pooling your resources, you can put together a good crew and hire someone to run sound and lights who's familiar with all the groups.

If you don't have roadies, consider helping each other out. If you're a guitar player there's nothing wrong with being the guitar tech for one of the other bands before or after your set. They can return the favor when it's your turn.

Also, rather than having each band trying to sell its own CDs and merchandise from the back of the room, you can have one big table for all the groups, just like at the big concerts.

If you're playing for the door, you probably know it's a good idea to have someone on your team working the door with his or her own counter. But you may not always have someone you can spare to leave on the door all night. Now you will. With four or more groups working together, one or two people can cover the door for everyone.

Another variation on this theme, especially for a temporary mastermind group, is to choose members from groups in one or two nearby cities. Then book shows in each city. The hometown bands get to headline in their respective cities. You can also bus or get your fans to caravan to the neighboring cities so you've got a good crowd at all the gigs.

This is a great way to broaden your fan base and expand your circle of gigs. It's also a win-win for all the bands involved. More legwork is involved, but you can still combine resources and print one poster for all the gigs.

How you organize all this is up to your mastermind group. One of the first things you'll want to do when forming your group is make a list of all the skills, equipment, and resources available to each group member.

Let's say one member's bass player is also a graphic designer. Or maybe the singer's boyfriend works for a screen printing company. If so, then let that group be in charge of designing the posters.

One of the groups involved might own a killer sound system and light show as well as a good-size truck. Maybe this group's primary responsibility will be stage management, production, and transportation.

Things may not divide out evenly, but can you see the general idea here? It all starts with taking an inventory of each group's resources, both human and material.

If you're a solo artist, this plan can still work. If you normally perform solo, get together with five or six other acoustic acts. If you're a singer who needs a backing group, form a group of singers. You can hire sidemen to be the backing band for the entire show, with each of you performing an entire set or just several songs each.

I've focused primarily on a live event scenario here, but there are far more potential benefits for a musician mastermind group. You could record a CD in a similar fashion, with each group having two or three cuts.

Or it can be something as simple as this. Let's say you need a new bass player. Rather than just relying on the people you know to find a replacement, you can call on your mastermind group to help and suddenly have a much larger group of people helping you find that replacement.

You can compare notes with other members about what certain clubs are paying, which agents are ripping off bands, where to find great deals on gear, and which local journalists are friendly to local artists.

Far too many musicians form a jealous rivalry with other bands and never cooperate. That's a huge mistake. When bands work together, the music community always grows stronger. That happened in Seattle with the grunge bands in the early '90s, the hair bands in LA and funk bands in Minneapolis in the '80s, and in other music hotbeds over the years.

Form a musician mastermind group now and you'll be amazed by the results.

27

MASTERMINDING FOR INTERNET MARKETERS

Bill Hibbler

Internet marketing is the primary theme of our current mastermind group, the Wimberley Group.

A mastermind can be beneficial for anyone, but there are additional benefits for those who make their living online. Internet marketers usually work out of a home office, which means we tend to be isolated. Our customers and peers are all over the world, but we rarely meet them in person. Usually, the only time we have any face-to-face contact is at live seminars.

So, in addition to all the other benefits, the group meetings are also a social setting for us. But there are lots of other benefits to an Internet marketing mastermind.

In our group, members have created products together (including this book), spoken at each other's live seminars and teleseminars, and promoted each other's products to our mailing lists.

Besides doing joint ventures, there are a number of resources that can be shared:
- Web site designers
- Graphic designers

- Web site automation services
- Virtual assistants
- Product fulfillment companies
- Print-on-demand publishers
- Teleseminar and web conferencing services
- Online audio and video software and services
- Programmers
- Autoresponder services
- Coregistration services

And the list goes on and on. Rather than using cheap shared hosting, members can go in on a dedicated server for your web sites. Instead of paying $20 a month to a company where your web site shares a server with hundreds or even thousands of other sites, for about the same money, five or six of you can share a fast, state-of-the-art web server, which means your web sites will load faster for visitors and are far less likely to have down time.

You can also compare notes on joint venture partners, affiliate software, ebook software, Internet marketing courses, and other software.

In our group, we give feedback on product and service ideas, brainstorm book titles, and review each other's sales letters and even e-mails.

As this book is being written, we've had the Wimberley Group for nearly two years. In that time, I have seen my annual sales increase by over 270 percent! Although that's not entirely due to forming this mastermind group, I'd say it's the single most significant factor due to joint ventures, coauthored products, and the power of the mastermind.

I suggest that you initially list your collective skills and resources. Is one of you a techie? Does one member have excellent graphic skills? Is one a great writer? Make a list. And make sure to include not only members' skills. If someone in the group has found a reliable service provider, that's great—put him or her on the list.

For resources, you want to compare notes about what credit card merchant companies you're using, what shopping cart system, hosting companies, and so on. The idea is to expand your individual resource list to a group resource list with everything you could possibly need in your online business.

The next thing you should do is have each member write a brief bio and description of his or her online business, including a list of current web sites and current products and services. Also, include current contact info. If your group meets in person, make enough copies for everyone in the group. If you meet online or by phone, get this information to the group via e-mail or fax.

Once you get started, the sky's the limit. You can promote each other's products to your mailing lists. You can coauthor ebooks, create software products, interview each other for audio products and teleseminars, and put on live seminars together. The possibilities are unlimited.

Let's say you've struggled to find joint venture partners and have only one or two. A mastermind group can bring you five or six new partners just from among the group members. And if each member comes into the group with two or three good JV partners, then you could potentially have a pool of 20 or more JV partners if your group members are willing to make an introduction.

If you're in Internet marketing, I highly recommend forming a mastermind group right away, whether it be an online, telephone, or in-person group.

28

MASTERMINDING FOR CHRISTIANS

Elena Hibbler

Somewhere I heard that the first mastermind group recorded in the annals of history was Jesus and His disciples. It was a very powerful one, too, for together they changed the world! It is interesting that God Himself said in the Bible that where two or three gather in His name, He will be with them. So, God Himself credits the importance of a mastermind.

Christendom has long adopted the idea of mastermind groups (without necessarily calling them so) in the form of prayer groups, family group meetings, and spiritual accountability groups. Some of my most special and strongest friendships were formed in the comfort of someone's home as we gathered each Friday to share our thoughts and revelations about the word of God, to pray together, or to encourage and support others. There is a special beauty about assembling in a group of likeminded people, and even though we did not always have a certain goal aside from fellowship and worship in mind, we always left the meeting enriched. Much of my knowledge of the Bible comes from these meetings.

But the most exciting and the most unusual mastermind that I have been part of is not a conventional church family group, it is an online group called "Meetings in the Upper Room." About a year ago I discovered a web site advertising an unusual project for Russian-speaking Christians from all over the world. A few years earlier, Pastor Pavel, a pastor of a small church in St. Petersburg, Russia, had decided to share his teaching, which was extremely well received in his church, with other believers online. The project grew and became very popular.

There are no prerequisites to join a group; all it takes is your willingness to become part of the group and share some information about yourself with the other participants. Once about 15 people applied, our group was ready to take off.

Our leader, this same pastor from St. Petersburg, sends out his lecture and everyone is to write a response, usually within the next two weeks. The responses are sent by e-mail and then shared among the group and the leader. Anyone wanting to comment on others' ideas is welcome to. To round off the discussion on one topic, the leader writes extensive comments that usually motivate us to do more research on the topic.

All that is asked of the participants is sincerity and their own opinions on the topic. Because the topics discussed are always very controversial, the response is incredible: Everyone has something to say. The goal is to see yourself in the mirror of the Bible. If in the first few letter exchanges people tend to be very careful about expressing their views, within a couple of months they begin to open up. The rules get stricter as we go along. If someone fails to respond on time, the privilege of being part of the group is temporarily suspended until he or she catches up. Ordinarily, when the group turns into a real mastermind instead of the initial group of strangers, we have about six to eight active participants. Besides our usual letter exchange, we all gather on an online forum where we discuss the most urgent questions and just get to know each other better.

With all that said, let me share some of the incredible benefits and advantages of participating in such a group.

- The most obvious one for me is finding a church home. Have you ever heard of an online church? I've been looking for kindred spirits in my walk with God ever since I first moved to the United States in 2002. I've found them now among my compatriots, many of whom are scattered around the world.

- Another significant advantage is that I've found the mentor and spiritual leader I've always wanted. I need to emphasize that the leader's role in such a group is vitally important. He's the one who selects the curriculum for our discussion. He's the one who has authority to stop any unnecessary arguments or diversions from the topic. We've had people quit because they thought the rules were too strict, but everyone who chooses to stay and play by the rules benefits greatly. The leader's role is especially important in the early stages of the group formation, as he sets the tone and atmosphere of every meeting. Only if people feel that they can trust the leader can they start trusting each other.

- "Meetings in the Upper Room" has helped me solve many spiritual questions that I've had for years. Some of my closest friends have remarked that they've seen a great change in my character and personality ever since I joined the group. That alone makes it worth participating!

- As we've grown closer, in our private communication we've begun to discuss all kinds of issues, not just spiritual ones. Several businessmen in our group have even found great new ways to expand their businesses by brainstorming with other group members.

- I personally have received great support from my teammates of the ministry that God entrusted me with: helping orphans in my hometown in Russia. Many Russian kids wouldn't have had Christmas gifts last year but for the loving support of a few of my group members.

- Several of us have decided to join the church in St. Petersburg and help Pastor Pavel's ministry in any way we can. That is a significant benefit for the church!

Last fall many of the members of our meetings met in person in St. Petersburg for the first time. What a joyous time it was! Everyone commented on how this ministry has helped them find themselves and a new meaning in life. It's a commitment and a great investment of time, but all the spiritual and emotional fruit we reap makes it worthwhile!

Spiritual mastermind groups won't necessarily make you wealthy materially, but they will certainly enrich your spiritual life and, hopefully, give you a sense of acceptance and love that we are always looking for.

29

MASTERMINDING FOR SOFTWARE DEVELOPERS

Calvin Chipman[4]

I like to do things on my own. However, I have learned that no great success can be accomplished without the application of the mastermind principle. As I understand it, the mastermind principle is to combine the efforts of two or more people to accomplish a desired result. I use this principle for nearly everything I do.

As a software developer, I use the mastermind principle throughout the process to create the final product. Let me go through the process of developing a software product to show how I use the principle.

The idea for a project either begins in my mind or with someone bringing the idea to me. When someone brings the idea to me, that is the beginning of the mastermind principle at work. By discussing

---

[4] Calvin H. Chipman is president of Chipman Custom Software, Inc., and general manager of MyEasySoftware, LLC.

the idea, we both come up with better ideas of how to implement based on our collective experience.

When developing an idea on my own, I also solicit the ideas of several other people before embarking on the project. The collective ideas and opinions of several people always improve on the original idea.

Sometimes financial resources are required to create the software. Investors or partners are found and add their suggestions for the creation of the product. Attorneys and accountants are used to assure that all legal and financial aspects of the venture are covered.

During the development process, there are parts that may be new to me or may be outside the range of my expertise. If what is unknown can easily be learned, then I research who can teach me what I don't know and learn from another person's experience. That may come from talking with other developers, researching on the Internet, or finding a book that provides the necessary information. If the unknown parts would take too long to learn, then I enlist the help of experts by hiring them to do the work or making them partners in the project. The collective work of all involved creates the end result.

Upon completion of the development process, a testing phase begins. During the testing phase, several people are asked to use the software and provide feedback on their testing experience. Those collective suggestions are then incorporated into the product to improve the software.

When the software is completed, the marketing is done by another team of individuals who have expertise in that area.

The expertise of many people is involved to bring to pass even the simplest software application. More complex software requires the collective work of even more people.

I learned a long time ago from my own experience that one person cannot do everything—even though I may want to. It is only by using the experience of other people that we can make progress. When we create something that can be used now and in the future, we are also helping others along the pathway of life.

All of the modern conveniences that we enjoy today are the result of the collective work of past inventors and workers. As a recipient of these conveniences, I feel that we each have an obligation to help others—now and in the future—by using the mastermind principle to improve things even more. It is a way of saying thanks by doing the same for others.

The Beginning

You've read how to create and run your own mastermind. You've also heard from others, offering you their opinions and advice.

Here's what we suggest you do next:
1. State your goal. What kind of mastermind group do you want? For what purpose?
2. Create a plan. How will you look for members?
3. Take the first step. Take action. Announce the first meeting. Invite people. Get the ball rolling.

Masterminds can bring you health, wealth, romance—and so much more. Have fun, and keep us posted on the adventure. Enjoy!

Resources

Brecher, Natalie. *Profit from the Power of Many: How to Use Mastermind Teams to Create Success.* Altamonte Springs, FL: Cheetah Express, 2004.

Canfield, Jack. *The Success Principles.* New York: Harper-Collins, 2005.

Franklin, Benjamin. *The Autobiography of Benjamin Franklin.* New York: Touchstone, 2003.

Hansen, Mark Victor, and Robert G. Allen. *Cracking the Millionaire Code: Your Key to Enlightened Wealth.* New York: Harmony Books, 2005.

Hansen, Mark Victor and Robert G. Allen. *The One Minute Millionaire: The Enlightened Way to Wealth.* New York: Harmony Books, 2002.

Hibbler, Bill, and Dr. Joe Vitale. *The Ultimate Guide to Creating Moneymaking Ebooks.* Wimberley, TX: Gigtime Media, 2004.

Hill, Napoleon. *The Law of Success.* Meriden, CT: Ralston University Press, 1928.

Hill, Napoleon. *Think and Grow Rich.* New York: Ballantine Books (reissue), 1987.

Menand, Louis. *The Metaphysical Club: A Story of Ideas in America.* New York: Farrar, Straus and Giroux, 2001.

Sher, Barbara, and Annie Gotlieb. *Teamworks: Building Support Groups That Guarantee Success.* New York: Warner Books, 1989.

Surowiecki, James. *The Wisdom of Crowds.* New York: Doubleday, 2005.

Vitale, Joe. *The Attractor Factor: 5 Easy Steps for Creating Wealth (or Anything Else) from the Inside Out.* Hoboken, NJ: John Wiley & Sons, 2005.

Vitale, Joe. *There's a Customer Born Every Minute.* Hoboken, NJ: John Wiley & Sons, 2006.

About the Authors

Joe Vitale is the author of way too many books to list here, from *The Attractor Factor* to *There's a Customer Born Every Minute* to *Life's Missing Instruction Manual.* He has been in numerous masterminds and credits a weight loss of 80 pounds to one of them. His main web site is www.mrfire.com. His corporate site is www.hypnoticMarketingInc.com.

Bill Hibbler is the owner of Gigtime Media, an Internet marketing consulting firm. He runs several successful web sites, including www.EcommerceConfidential.com, www.Create-Ultimate-Ebooks.com, www.InfoProductU.com, and www.RudlReport.com.

Bill is a former successful artist manager and tour manager in the music industry (Humble Pie, Deep Purple's Glenn Hughes, and many others). He started a commercial sound system rental company and vintage guitar business at the ripe old age of 15. Clients included The Who, Aerosmith, Bad Company, Van Halen, Dire Straits, Nazareth, Chuck Berry, and Pat Benatar.

Bill's first ebook, *The Rudl Report,* has been a big hit with readers, who learn how to save money on Internet marketing products and services and enjoy Bill's honest, unbiased reviews. He's also coauthored *The Ultimate Guide to Creating Moneymaking Ebooks* with Joe Vitale.

Bill has contributed to numerous books, including Joe Vitale's *The Attractor Factor* and *The E-Code,* Pat

O'Bryan's *The Myth of Passive Income,* and Jan Goldberg's *Real People Working in Entertainment.*

Bill has founded two very successful mastermind groups. The first five-member group in Houston, Texas, was composed of local musicians and music business owners. Within a year, members of the group had major label recording contracts, spots on high-profile concert tours, a new recording studio, and, in Bill's case, an artist management contract with a multiplatinum recording artist.

Bill's current mastermind group consists of seven Internet marketers, including best-selling authors Joe Vitale and Cindy Cashman *(Everything Men Know about Women, You're Fired: 17 Things You Can Do to Help Speed Up the Process).* In the past 18 months, members have seen their income skyrocket and credit joining the group as a major factor in their success.

Special Free Gift from the Authors

FREE

Here's How You Can Get Your $95.85 Value Mastermind Starter Kit

As our personal thank you for reading this book, we'd like to offer you a very special gift. To help you start and run your own successful mastermind group as soon as possible, we've created this special starter kit.

You get:

- Interview, member contact, and background info forms to help you get your group up and running quickly and easily. ($9.95 Value)
- Member report form to track your progress and keep the group abreast of your activities. Helps members stay focused so you can accomplish more in less time. Includes instructions on how to customize the form for your particular group's industry or focus. ($29.00 Value)
- Meet & Grow Rich Audio Presentation. An overview of Bill and Joe's Mastermind Success System and highlights of interviews with successful entrepreneurs. ($37.00 Value)
- Mastermind Technology Resource Report. Details on the latest technology for running your telephone or online mastermind. ($9.95 Value)

- Information on where to find potential members for your local, telephone, or online mastermind group. ($9.95 Value)

To obtain this Free Mastermind Kit immediately: Please visit us online at http://www.MeetAndGrowRich.com/MAGR.

Front Cover Flap

Succeeding at work and life is no easy task. Often it feels like it's you against the world. But what would it be like if you had a support group that could advise, encourage, and inspire you? What if this support group could help you focus on your goals and achieve them faster? Would you take advantage of such a group, if it existed?

If you don't know about mastermind groups, *Meet and Grow Rich* is a great introduction to them. A mastermind group is a powerful alliance between people who help support and enlighten each other on the road to success. However, it's much more than a support group for like-minded people. Mastermind groups bring together individuals who share the same goals and dreams and work together to achieve them. Though this book focuses primarily on using mastermind groups for achieving wealth and financial freedom, mastermind groups can be developed to focus on almost anything—from hobbies to spirituality to personal relationships. The only limit to what you can do with a mastermind group is your own imagination.

Meet and Grow Rich shows you how an effective mastermind group works, how to create and operate one yourself, and how to use it as a stepping stone to financial success. You'll discover how great entrepreneurs like Andrew Carnegie and William Wrigley Jr. used mastermind groups to achieve profound success and how you can follow in their footsteps to achieve your own version of spectacular success.

In addition to comprehensive coverage of the ins and outs of mastermind groups, this complete resource includes tips and tactics from a long list of contributors with firsthand expert knowledge of the subject. No matter what your passion—from making money to making art—you'll find here all the expert advice and proven guidance you need to form your own inspiring, enlightening, and supportive mastermind group.

Back Cover Flap

JOE VITALE is President of Hypnotic Marketing, Inc., a marketing consulting firm. He has been called "the Buddha of the Internet" for his combination of spirituality and marketing acumen. His articles are widely read, and his professional clients include the American Red Cross, Memorial Hermann Children's Hospital, and many other small and large international businesses. He is also the author of *The E-Code, The Attractor Factor,* and *Life's Missing Instruction Manual,* all from Wiley. For more information, see Joe's Web site at www.MrFire.com.

BILL HIBBLER is the owner of Gigtime Media, an Internet marketing consulting firm. He is the founder and director of www.MeetandGrowRich.com; coauthor of several bestselling e-books; and the publisher of *E-Commerce Confidential,* a newsletter for online marketers.

Back Cover Material

**praise for
MEET & GROW RICH**

"I'm a big fan of mastermind groups. I've used them for over thirty years and know the power they provide everyone in such a group. I'm delighted to see this inspiring, easy-to-follow manual. Read it and follow what it suggests."
—Jack Canfield

co-creator of the Chicken Soup for the Soul® series and bestselling author of *The Success Principles*™

"Absolutely the best practical guide to creating, profiting, and growing your business with your own mastermind group. A must-read for anyone who wants to succeed in ANY business!"
—Jim Edwards

author and speaker (www.ebookfire.com)

"I have been part of various mastermind groups for over twenty years that have easily made me millions. Without a doubt this book is the most advanced defi nitive guide to why and how any serious human should be a part of one."
—John Assaraf

cofounder, OneCoach (www.onecoach.com)

Books For ALL Kinds of Readers

At ReadHowYouWant we understand that one size does not fit all types of readers. Our innovative, patent pending technology allows us to design new formats to make reading easier and more enjoyable for you. This helps improve your speed of reading and your comprehension. Our EasyRead printed books have been optimized to improve word recognition, ease eye tracking by adjusting word and line spacing as well as minimizing hyphenation. Our EasyRead SuperLarge editions have been developed to make reading easier and more accessible for vision-impaired readers. We offer Braille and DAISY formats of our books and all popular E-Book formats.

We are continually introducing new formats based upon research and reader preferences. Visit our web-site to see all of our formats and learn how you can Personalize our books for yourself or as gifts. Sign up to Become A RHYW Registered Reader.

www.readhowyouwant.com

Made in the USA
Lexington, KY
30 March 2015